★ ★

AMERICA'S STORY
Book 2: Forming a New Nation

Dear Student,

In Book 2 of *America's Story,* we're going to take part in a revolution—America's War for Independence and the creation of our Constitution.

We'll cross the icy Delaware River with George Washington in order to surprise the British. We'll join two young women who are determined to stop a British messenger. We'll even hear the other side of the story as we eavesdrop on two British officers trying to understand how their powerful army was defeated by the American Patriots.

The War for Independence was a test of character for many people in many ways. We'll read about a brother and a sister who become enemies, about Benjamin Franklin seeking help from the French, and about a patriotic teenage girl who must decide what really happened at the Boston Massacre.

The birth of America was not easy. Those years were filled with adventure, danger, heroism, and patriotism on both sides. There will be true stories about famous people whose names you'll recognize immediately, and other stories that are based on fact but told through the voices of fictional people. Through these stories, you'll gain a new appreciation for America's early settlers and for the way of life you enjoy today.

David C King

Copyright © 1996 Sundance Publishing
234 Taylor Street, Littleton, MA 01460

This revision is based on the original manuscript by David C. King.

The portraits on pages 26 and 28 have been reproduced from the *Dictionary of American Portraits,* published by Dover Publications, Inc., 1967.

ISBN 0-7608-0476-1
10 9 8 7 6 5 4 3 2 1 DS

Table of Contents

Redcoats and Colonials

How did the colonists and the British work together during the French and Indian War?

Background

The year was 1757. People in the American colonies were worried. Those who lived in outlying areas feared for their lives. Great Britain and France were at war. The Thirteen Colonies were bound to be caught up in it. After all, the colonies were part of the British Empire. And this was also a war for control of North America.

In Book 1, the story "Clash of Empires" tells how the war started in the American wilderness. It also describes the part played by young George Washington. This was the conflict Americans call the French and Indian War. In Europe, it is remembered as the Seven Years' War.

During 1756 and 1757, nothing seemed to go right for the British. They lost battles to the French in Europe, in distant India, and on the high seas. In North America, the British and the colonial militia lost one battle after another. From Maine to Georgia, frontier settlements were open to attack by France's Native American allies.

Then, in 1758, William Pitt became leader of the British Parliament. He presented a bold new plan for winning the war. The

British would no longer try to win everywhere at the same time, he declared. Instead, they would pour everything into the war for North America. Once France was defeated there, Pitt was sure the French Empire would collapse.

The colonists were thrilled with the new war strategy. Their coastline was now protected by British ships. Instead of a few hundred British soldiers, thousands of the famous Redcoats arrived. The colonial militia were eager to fight alongside the Redcoats.

Here are two letters from a 16-year-old militia soldier from Kingston, New York. The letters tell about his adventures in two of the most important battles of the French and Indian War.

July 26, 1759

$\mathcal{D}$*ear Mother and Father,*

Yesterday, we had our first taste of battle and we won! We have taken Fort Niagara from the French.

Right at the start, let me assure you that I am fine. I am unscratched, healthy, and well fed. I feel strong enough to lift Mrs. Kleinschmidt's ox.

Now, let me describe the Battle of Niagara as clearly as I can. As a prologue, we spent several weeks marching across the western wilderness of New York Colony. This in itself was a battle. Our enemies were weariness, the fierce heat, thunderstorms, and the rugged land. Oh, yes, and huge black flies that could bite deep enough to draw blood. Some of the men dropped out of the march, their feet impossibly swollen or blistered. It is not surprising. By the time we reached Niagara, Tad Parsons and I calculated we had walked four hundred miles.

During this hike, we learned that we Colonials were the main army. Everyone was excited about that. All the other battles recently have been led by the British. It almost seemed they did not believe militia soldiers could fight. At Niagara, we would have a chance to prove what we could do. The British would help with just two regiments plus two ships out on the lake. The battle for the fort was ours to win or lose.

Our army numbered about sixteen hundred. There were dozens of different militia units, some from almost every colony. At Lake Oswego, we were placed under the command of General William Johnson. He is the man, I hear, who convinced the Iroquois to be on our side.

A few men grumbled about marching and fighting alongside the Iroquois. After all, hardly a New York settlement has been spared the fury of their raids. But now they are allies. And, as Tad said, "I'd rather fight next to them than against them." It struck me later, too, that the Iroquois as enemies would have blocked our march across New York.

As we neared Niagara, Iroquois runners made contact with the British. Our Captain Hawthorne told us the plan of attack. The Redcoats would attack the fort from the south, along the Niagara River. We would attack from the east, following the shore of Lake Ontario. The two British warships would start the battle with a bombardment at dawn.

We moved into position at night. Through gaps in the clouds, the moonlight revealed the outlines of the fort. It looked massive and strong. And it was very close—

THE ROAD TO INDEPENDENCE

only about four hundred yards away. Few men slept well that night. We were all nervous and jumpy.

As the first light streaked the sky, we heard the cannons booming from the ships. We could see the shots arc through the air and crash into the fort.

Two hours later we saw the British off to our left. They were marching to the attack. They were in perfect formation, and the drummers kept up a steady beat. Captain Hawthorne had told us this was how armies fought in Europe. Armies attacked in formation across open fields. They did not break ranks even as shots fell.

Of course, we attacked like the Iroquois. We made use of every bush and tree, every hill and gully for protection. As we advanced, only two cannons were firing at us. From that, we could tell that the French thought the British soldiers were the main army. Even so, I did not find it easy to advance toward those cannons. The small shot the cannons fired often buzzed past us like swarms of angry bees.

Before I knew it, I was one of the first scaling the wall. When we reached the top, there were no defenders to challenge us. We were on a grassy hill. The cannons that had fired on us were in a tunnel under the hill. The green-clad French were all manning posts facing the British or the ships. Some, with the help of some Huron [a Native American group], were at the gate, ready to charge the Redcoats.

We crouched and waited for more of our men and the Iroquois to climb up. Captain Hawthorne dropped down next to me and handed me a neatly folded flag.

"Run this up that flagpole, Bill," he whispered. "I'll guard you. The fort is ours."

The flagpole was near the top of the hill. With the Captain crouched in front of me, I pulled down the French flag. Then I hooked on the British Union Jack and raised it up the pole. As the

British flag flapped open in the morning breeze, our men let out a cheer and charged down into the fort. The French soldiers and the Huron wheeled around in surprise. They saw at once that their situation was hopeless.

Minutes later the Battle of Niagara was over. Some of our men opened the gate to let in the British. They looked relieved that they were greeted by us and not a French counterattack.

Last night we celebrated the victory with the British. The cooks prepared a feast. They used the best supplies from the French officers' kitchen. And I heard some British officers say that we Colonials had fought a brilliant battle. They said this may be the greatest victory in the war so far. With the water routes blocked, the French will not be able to supply their western forts.

I will write again soon. Our ninety-day enlistments are nearly over. I shall surely be home for the first harvest.

Affectionately, your son,

William "Bill" Demaret

September 24, 1759

Dear Mother and Father,

I trust that Tad Parsons has arrived safely back in Kingston. By now he will have told you that I volunteered for another ninety days.

I think you will understand why I could not resist. At Niagara, the British told us about the next campaign. A Lieutenant Hastings said, "We are going to attack Quebec. It is the capital of New France and France's most powerful fort. It is also the headquarters for their military commander, General Montcalm. Let me assure you all, whoever wins at Quebec, wins the war."

Then he asked General Johnson for two hundred Colonial volunteers. They would be serving on a special mission. Many volunteered. Since I am only sixteen, I did not expect to be chosen. But I was one of the first picked! Captain Hawthorne was named to lead us.

On this expedition, our task was to create a diversion—to put the French off guard. We were to circle around behind the city. We would attack just before the British attacked from the other side. As we climbed aboard one of the British warships, all the Americans were excited. This was going to be the greatest battle ever fought in North America. And we were to be part of it.

I wish you both had been here to see it. Since we were behind the city, we only understood the battle afterward. Even then, you would have been as amazed as we were.

Quebec is a walled city, like a great fortress. It sits on a mighty wall of rock overlooking the St. Lawrence River. When you are on the river, the cliff appears as a straight wall rising two hundred feet to the city. It looked impossible to scale. But British scouts kept studying it until they found a narrow path. They planned to take an army up that uncertain path.

This bold scheme was the plan of General James Wolfe. People said he was the best of the British generals. And yet he was only thirty-one years old. Wolfe had sailed up the St. Lawrence River with a huge invasion fleet—there were one hundred and sixty-eight ships, and those ships carried nine thousand Redcoats, ready for battle.

The part we Colonials played was small but important. Three hours before Wolfe's assault was to start, we attacked Quebec from the west. Captain Hawthorne had told us to keep moving. "Shoot as fast as you can load," he said. "We may trick them into turning some of their defenses away from the river."

The trick worked quite well. Within an hour, we saw several hundred of those familiar green uniforms on top of the walls. We learned later that Wolfe had ordered other diversions both up and down the river. French troops were rushing in all directions looking for the main attack.

Suddenly the air was filled with the sound of cannon and musket fire. It came from the other side of the fort, near the cliff. Thousands of guns seemed to be going off at once. The main battle had begun.

That battle was fought on a level field at the top of the cliff. Climbing at night, forty-five hundred British had managed to climb that path. Wolfe himself was there, leading a squadron of his best men. Instead of attacking the fort, he waited for the French to attack him. And that was what Montcalm, the French general, did.

Montcalm directed the attack against Wolfe's Redcoats. The armies clashed on that open field. They were now fighting European-style—two armies in perfect formation. The Redcoats said later that Wolfe waited and waited to give the order to fire. The French were less than forty yards away when he finally gave the order.

The chess game between Montcalm and Wolfe was over. The French lines wavered, and then the

4

THE ROAD TO INDEPENDENCE

men ran in full retreat. Montcalm tried to rally them as they fled, but he was felled by a British shot. He died shortly after.

The British had won the major battle of the war. But they, too, lost their leader. Wolfe was badly wounded early in the battle. He lived just long enough to learn he had won.

Now, I am ready to come home. I have seen enough of war to last me a lifetime. This war with France is almost over now. It has been a great triumph for Great Britain. But I am also proud of how much we Colonials contributed. Now with Great Britain in control of Canada, we should have peace.

Homeward bound, your son,

William "Bill" Demaret

STORY NOTES

At the outbreak of the French and Indian War, the British colonies were nestled along the east coast. Compared to the land claimed by the French—which included more than half of what we now consider the United States, and most of Canada—the British colonies were very small. But they had many more colonists than did the French. After the fall of Quebec, it was clear that the British side had won the war. In the peace treaty, France turned over to the British all the lands west of the Appalachian Mountains to the Mississippi and all of Canada.

William Demaret's story and letters are fictional. But the events surrounding the battles of Niagara and Quebec are true.

THE ROAD TO INDEPENDENCE

Word Study

For each word in the left column, write the letter of the correct definition in the right column. Then, on a separate sheet of paper, write new sentences using each of the underlined words.

_____ 1. The colonists fought as a <u>militia</u>, not in the regular British army.

a. introduction or beginning part

_____ 2. As a <u>prologue</u> to the battle, we loaded our guns.

b. period of time in military service

_____ 3. I <u>calculated</u> that we had walked over four hundred miles.

c. group of soldiers or military units

_____ 4. The British army lined up in a perfect <u>formation</u> to wait for the attack.

d. a journey for a specific purpose

_____ 5. The high cliff was difficult to <u>scale</u>.

e. citizens who fight with the army in emergencies

_____ 6. The British organized their <u>campaign</u> against the French in North America.

f. climb a steep incline

_____ 7. A Colonial's <u>enlistment</u> lasted ninety days.

g. a distraction to draw attention from something

_____ 8. The soldiers crossed New York and into Canada on the <u>expedition</u>.

h. something organized or arranged in lines or columns

_____ 9. We created a <u>diversion</u> so that the French didn't see the British coming.

i. figured out or estimated by reason

_____10. The small <u>squadron</u> won an important victory.

j. a series of military battles

Story Facts and Ideas

In a short paragraph for each of the following, tell why . . .

1. Bill raised the Union Jack instead of the American flag after the capture of Fort Niagara.

2. the capture of Fort Niagara was so important to the British army.

3. the British generals wanted two hundred Colonial volunteers to remain with the army.

4. William Demaret wanted to join the campaign for Quebec.

5. the battle at Quebec was such an important victory for the British.

Questions to Talk and Write About

1. William Pitt decided to try to defeat the French in North America. The British would not fight the French anywhere else in the world. Why do you think Pitt made that decision? Why was it a wise one?

2. What was the role of the Iroquois in the war against the French? What did some militia soldiers think about fighting on the same side as the Iroquois? Why? Why didn't the Iroquois join other Native American groups on the side of the French?

3. Contrast the differences between the French and British way of fighting battles with the way the Colonials and Native Americans fought. Why do you think these differences existed? Which method do you think is better? Why?

4. Of the two battles described in this story, which do you think was the more difficult? Why? Which was more important? Why?

Things to Do

1. Use a map of New York State to trace William Demaret's route from the time he left Kingston, New York. The story will give you the clues you need. Find the best route to get him home after the Battle of Quebec. Then calculate how many miles he traveled from the beginning.

2. Carefully read the descriptions of the two battles. Then draw a battle plan or make a model of each battle. Show how the army approached, how the soldiers lined up, how the French defended, and so on.

3. These letters give us a few clues about William Demaret. Imagine you are a soldier fighting with Bill. Write a letter home telling what he is like.

4. Draw a map—or fill in an outline map—showing the North American lands controlled by Britain, France, and Spain before the war began. Then make a second map showing what Britain gained, what France lost, and what Spain lost and gained by the war. Use history and library books to find maps that will help.

5. Write or act out a scene not directly described in Bill's letters. For example:

   a. Mr. and Mrs. Demaret at home receiving one of their son's letters

   b. William and his friends talking in camp the night before a battle

   c. the French soldiers during the battle

The French and Indian War, 1756–1763

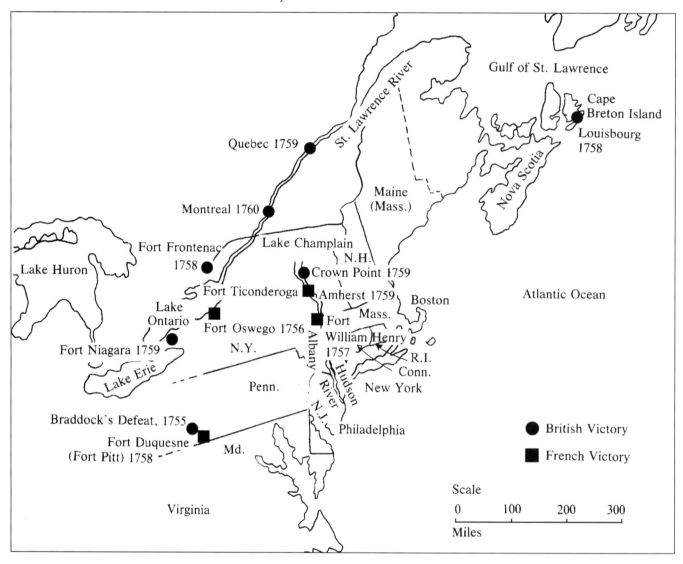

The Coming Storm

What part did Captain Thomas Preston play in the Boston Massacre?

I have been asked to write my own account of the event called the Boston Massacre. I was not present on that dreadful night of March 5, 1770. But I did know Captain Preston quite well. I did see him within minutes of the shooting.

Because Captain Preston is on trial for murder, I will be as accurate as I can. In all honesty, I swear that this is a true statement of what I remember.

Mercy Webster

For me, the story begins in September 1768, when I became fifteen. That was also the month when the two regiments of British soldiers arrived in Boston. They marched up King Street from the wharf and set up camp on the common. To us, it was as if a conquering army had entered our town.

Oh, how we hated those Redcoats! "Lobster-backs" people call them now. For the next year and a half, most people made the soldiers feel as unwelcome as they could without turning to violence.

Our troubles with the British started right after the victory over France in the French and Indian War. The war had been costly, and the British were in need of money at home. So they decided that the colonists should help pay for the British soldiers sent to protect the colonies, as well as the other officials who governed the colonies. Britain passed new taxes on items such as molasses, sugar,

To us, it was as if a conquering army had entered our town.

all legal documents, as well as newspapers, almanacs, and pamphlets. The worst part was that King George and the British Parliament had passed the taxes without giving the colonists any say in the matter. This was not fair.

Some of us decided to fight these unjust taxes. We joined groups called the Sons of Liberty and the Daughters of Liberty. We marched in protest parades and asked people to sign antitax petitions. All through the colonies, the Sons and Daughters of Liberty convinced people not to buy British goods. For the first time, we were really acting together—not as thirteen separate colonies.

Before long, trade with England fell by half. To save their own merchants, the British did away with almost all new taxes, except the one on tea. Our happiness, however, was short-lived.

Soon King George III and Parliament passed new taxes and went so far as to order the colonists in New York to open their homes to British soldiers. Can you imagine being forced to have a soldier, who has been sent by the king to enforce his

will on your friends and neighbors, sleeping and eating in your home? When New York Colony refused to obey, its Colonial Assembly was done away with. Every colony took this as a threat to its own liberties.

I mention all this so there can be no doubt about where I stand. I am a Daughter of Liberty, and my family are all Patriots. We have all been active in legal protests against the injustices of our King.

So you can imagine how angry we were when Captain Thomas Preston came to our home on January 5 of this year, 1770. We had been ordered to let a British officer stay in our home.

I was furious. "Just imagine it!" I fumed. "A Lobster-back living under our roof and sharing our food! This is an outrage!"

I was prepared to dislike Captain Preston long before I had met him. I thought he would be more like our jailer than our guest.

It was late on a stormy, wintry afternoon. I was in my room, enjoying the cozy warmth of my small fireplace. A pot of tea was steaming on the hearth. I was trying to work on my Greek lesson for school. But I could not keep my mind on studying. I kept thinking of this intruder coming to our home.

Just at that point I heard him at the front door, the heavy brass door-knocker echoing through the house. I hurried downstairs.

My parents and my brother Peter were standing at the door, waiting. The Captain was in the entryway. He stepped forward to introduce himself.

We were all stunned. For a moment, even my father was speechless. I guess we had been expecting one of those rough, rude soldiers we met on the streets so often.

Whatever the reason, we were caught off our guard by Captain Preston. He was a very handsome young man. As he introduced himself, I was struck by his correct speech and good manners.

He also looked at each of us in a direct, honest way that I knew my parents would like.

From that day on, none of us could hate Captain Preston. You can hate the actions of one country against your own. But when you meet a citizen of that country who is kind and friendly, the hatred disappears.

Captain Preston was with us exactly two months—until the day of the tragedy. During that period, there were times that I admired him. One morning, for instance, my brother and two of his friends were on their way to school when a gang of tough young men stopped them. The roughnecks blocked the way and would not let the boys pass.

It was Captain Preston who rescued them. He spotted the trouble as he was riding down the hill from our house. The boys still tell of how he jumped off his horse and confronted their tormentors straight on, causing the roughnecks to beat a swift retreat.

There were occasions, too, when I felt sorry for him. The street crowds in Boston never left the soldiers alone for long. They shouted insulting words at the Redcoats, taunted them, and even dared them to fight.

Twice I saw Captain Preston put up with the troublesome mob. On the second of these occasions, some began hurling bricks at the soldiers.

The Boston Massacre

Captain Preston began moving the men in a slow retreat. A paving stone struck one of the soldiers in the forehead with a sickening thud. The crowd vanished in seconds, knowing they had gone too far. The soldier was dead.

Thus, I did respect and even admire Captain Preston. But I could never forget that he was there to impose the king's will on us.

Our friend John Adams reminded us of this fact. He told us of seeing Captain Preston and some soldiers guarding a father and son named Saunders. The Saunderses were in chains and were being taken to prison. Old Saunders had known only one thing all his life—how to make excellent rum. Now he was going to prison for using smuggled sugar. Adams, who acted as their lawyer, said that Saunders could not even understand the crime.

I will mention one other incident, which my brother Peter told us of. A woman had slipped and fallen on the icy cobblestones outside the Customs House. The two Redcoats on guard ran to help her. But as soon as they reached her, someone shouted that the soldiers were trying to rob her. Within seconds, an angry mob had surrounded the two men.

My brother watched as Captain Preston ran out of the Customs House to assist his men. With his pistol and sword drawn, he forced the mob to back up. He and the two sentries then backed slowly into the Customs House.

When he had finished the story, Peter added, "The frightening thing was the look on the Captain's face. This was not the gentle, polite man whose company we enjoy. I know now that he will shoot if he must."

Mother shivered at the thought. "For months now," she said, "I have felt like we've been living with an approaching storm. The clouds begin to gather and the sky darkens. The wind is hushed. You know it is only a matter of time . . ." She sighed. "I think those soldiers have brought the storm much closer."

Late on the evening of March 5, 1770, Captain Preston barged through the front door. My parents, Peter, and I were jolted out of the quiet mood of the drawing room. I could hear the Captain struggling to remove his cape.

The moment I saw him, I knew there was something wrong. Captain Preston could not get the cape off because his right arm hung uselessly. Around his head was a bandage. His tunic was splattered with mud, and one sleeve was nearly torn off.

He started to speak, but Mother hushed him. Peter helped him with his cloak and tunic. Father gave him a tumbler of brandy. I fetched linen for bandages while Mother went for the hot water kettle on the kitchen hearth.

Within a few minutes, his arm was in a sling and a proper bandage covered his gashed ear. He thanked us but then stood up and moved a little away from us.

"There has been an awful tragedy tonight," he said. "I wanted you to hear it first from me. Five of your fellow citizens lie dead tonight. Two others are wounded. The men were not armed."

I stared at him, trying to understand. I had worried about trouble. But how could unarmed men be shot down? I wanted to know what had happened.

"I shall be blamed for this," he said calmly. "I was the officer in charge. But I swear to you that I never gave an order to shoot. How can I ask you to believe me? And yet I must. I can only offer my most solemn oath that no order was given."

We all agreed that we would listen to his account. He began by telling us how one of the troublesome crowds was picking on the ten soldiers guarding the Customs House in which various tax collectors worked. Others heard the shouting and sent for Captain Preston. By the time the Captain arrived, the crowd had become louder and bolder.

12

THE ROAD TO INDEPENDENCE

"We faced a mob of over a hundred. They were shouting and cursing. Boys were throwing snowballs, many with rocks in them. Some of the men were armed with boards or clubs.

"I had my men fix bayonets, and that threat drove the crowd back a little. But soon they were closing in again, knocking at the rifles or bayonets with their boards. My men were frightened but calm. One by one, I told each man to load—the first time I had ever done that.

"I then tried to reason with some of the crowd. I was standing now between my own men and the crowd.

"A young soldier behind me called to me. The instant I turned, one of the clubs hit me on the arm and a board smashed into my ear. I thought I was done for. I saw the young soldier who called get hit by a board. He staggered a step or two and his gun discharged.

"There seemed a moment there when time was frozen. The shot still seemed to echo through the night air. Then my men fired off a volley, and the crowd fled. The bodies of five colonists lay on the street. Three were dead, and the others close to death."

Many of the soldiers insisted they had heard someone shout "Fire!" But those closest to the Captain did not hear any order.

A sad, heavy silence fell over the room. I did not doubt his story. What was sad was that this good person had become the agent for something horrifying. This was the first blood shed between Great Britain and her colonies.

"On my way here," he added, "I learned that the city council has already met. I and eight of my men are to be arrested and tried for murder."

I was alarmed. "Father, we must do something to help Captain Preston get a fair trial. No one will want to help a British soldier. Do you think John Adams would be his lawyer?"

My father got up quickly and left the room just long enough to get his cape.

"I will get a message off to John Adams in Braintree," he said. "Captain Preston will need a good lawyer, and John is the best lawyer there is."

Captain Preston stood up. He looked very confused. "I don't understand," he said. "You are Patriots. Why would you be concerned with my trial?"

My father replied, "I intend to see to it that you have a fair trial. We must stand for liberty and justice in America. If we deny you your rights, then our ideals mean nothing."

STORY NOTES

John Adams did take the case, although many Patriots criticized him for it. The jury found Preston and his men not guilty. Two of the men received minor punishment for other crimes. The jury concluded that the mob started the affair, not the Captain. Adams would become the second president of the United States.

The first colonist to die at the Boston Massacre was a black sailor named Crispus Attucks. Some say that Attucks, who was a member of the Sons of Liberty, led the charge against the soldiers. The uproar surrounding the Boston Massacre forced the British to do away with most of the new taxes, but they continued to deny the colonists self-rule. One of the taxes that remained was that on tea, which would result in the Boston Tea Party.

The story is based on Captain Preston's journal. But the story of Preston being quartered at Mercy Webster's home is fiction.

THE ROAD TO INDEPENDENCE

Word Study

Fill in each blank with a word from the story. Then use your answers to fill in the boxes. Puzzle words are sentries, Assembly, tumbler, bayonets, tunic, regiment, taxes, Lobster, volley, patriot, colonists, Sons, Redcoats, Quartering.

1. Captain Preston ordered his men to fix their _____.

2. A _____ of shots was heard.

3. The British dissolved New York's Colonial _____.

4. A person who loves his or her country is a _____.

5. One group of protesters was the _____ of Liberty.

6. The _____ wanted to govern their own affairs.

7. The Captain drank from a _____.

8. The Patriots protested paying new _____.

9. Colonists called British soldiers _____ -backs.

10. Two _____ guarded the Customs House.

11. Preston's soldiers were _____.

12. The captain wore a red _____ over his shirt.

13. The _____ Act forced colonists to board British soldiers.

14. A British _____ came to keep order in Boston.

America's Story

Story Facts and Ideas

Explain the meaning and importance of these quotations from the story.

1. "Just imagine it," I fumed. "A Lobster-back living under our roof and sharing our food! This is an outrage!"

2. "For months now," she said, "I have felt like we've been living with an approaching storm."

3. "There has been an awful tragedy tonight," he said. . . . "I shall be blamed for this."

4. My father replied, "We must stand for liberty and justice in America. If we deny you your rights, then our ideals mean nothing."

Questions to Talk and Write About

1. Mercy and her family grew to like Captain Preston. But there were things about him that they did not like. Do you think Captain Preston was basically a good person? Or was he an evil person who acted nicely around the Websters? Explain.

2. How did the colonists treat the British soldiers? Why? How might the colonists have acted differently?

3. What type of person was Mercy Webster? Write a brief description of her.

4. In 1770, Boston was an exciting place. Would you like to have been living there at that time? Why or why not?

5. Who was to blame for the Boston Massacre, the Patriots or the British? Explain your answer.

Things to Do

1. Read an account of the Boston Massacre in an encyclopedia. What facts in the encyclopedia appear in this story? What facts are in the story that are not in the encyclopedia?

2. Imagine that you are Mercy Webster. Write an entry that you think she may have written in her diary. Tell how you feel about what is happening in Boston or at a Daughters of Liberty meeting.

3. Use an encyclopedia or a history book to find out more about a topic related to the American Revolution such as the Stamp Act, the Quartering Act, the Sons and Daughters of Liberty, or the Boston Tea Party.

4. Write a play about the trial of Captain Preston and the British soldiers. Classmates can take the roles of John Adams, witnesses, the judge, and the jury. What do you think went on at the trial?

A Lady's Farewell to Her Tea Table

A Lady's Farewell to Her Tea Table

Farewell the Teaboard with your gaudy attire,
Ye cups and saucers that I did admire;
To my cream pot and tongs I now bid adieu;
That pleasure's all fled that I once found in you . . .
No more shall my teapot so generous be
In filling the cups with this pernicious tea,
For I'll fill it with water and drink out the same,
Before I'll lose Liberty that dearest name . . .
Before she shall part I will die in the cause,
For I'll never be govern'd by tyranny's laws.

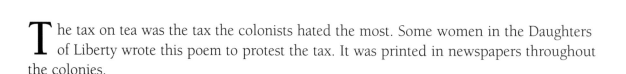

The tax on tea was the tax the colonists hated the most. Some women in the Daughters of Liberty wrote this poem to protest the tax. It was printed in newspapers throughout the colonies.

Questions/Activities

1. In your words, write the main idea of this poem.

2. This poem was written by the Daughters of Liberty to protest Britain's tax on tea. What did the Sons of Liberty do to protest this tax? What other things might the Sons and Daughters of Liberty have done?

3. Write a poem about the tea tax or about another event in the American Revolution. Or write a poem about something that you decide to give up for a good reason (such as candy or french fries). You may begin your poem with the words "Farewell my old favorite . . ."

THE ROAD TO INDEPENDENCE

The Battle of Loyalties

How did trouble between America and England turn a brother and a sister into enemies?

The first pale streaks of light had just appeared in the morning sky when Jordan Sherwood was jolted awake. He heard a familiar sound. Someone was cooling down a horse on the cobblestones in front of the carriage house. He knew it could mean only one thing. His younger sister Julia had finally come home.

Jordan was up and dressed in a matter of seconds. He glanced out the window and saw Julia walking slowly toward the kitchen door. She was wearing a Daughters of Liberty medallion. The sight of Julia's medallion added to the anger and bitterness Jordan had been feeling for weeks.

As he went down the stairs, Jordan made up his mind. His sister was no longer welcome in this house.

He found Julia in the kitchen. She was slumped, half-asleep, across the bench next to the hearth. The brother and sister greeted each other without warmth. There was no sign that they had not seen each other for months.

The room was still dark, so Jordan used his candle to light the wall sconces. Then he stoked up the fire for morning tea and porridge. Still standing, he turned to Julia.

"Julia, we must get this settled," he said sternly. "You have become a supporter of the Patriot cause, and your husband is a soldier in the Rhode Island militia. But this is a Loyalist household. We are loyal British subjects."

"Speak for yourself, Jordie," Julia answered. "I feel no loyalty to Britain or King George. They have been taking away our rights for years. Now we have to fight for justice."

Julia felt too worn out to argue like this. She had ridden all night in her eagerness to get home. All she wanted now was a decent meal and her old bed. But she could see that Jordan was not going to let her rest.

"I have every right to order you out of this house," Jordan said. His voice was cold and hard. "As the eldest, I am master here since Father died. But I don't want to order you out. I think it would be better if you left on your own. Right now is the best time. Mother is staying with Aunt Beth in Pawtucket and will be there another week. She need never know you came back."

Julia sat up and stared at her brother. She felt anger and tears rising within her. She had known they would argue when she came home to visit. But she had never expected anything like this.

"How can you do this?" she asked, trying to control the shakiness in her voice. "I thought this was our house. The Sherwood family house. What gives you the right to throw me out?"

She felt her mind spinning like a top. Her husband Alexander had just fought in the first major battle between the colonists and the British. He was fortunate to be alive, and now he was gone again. Why should she not come to her own home to rest? She had always listened to Jordie because he was the oldest. But she was twenty now and living her own life. She was proud of herself and her

The Boston Tea Party

THE ROAD TO INDEPENDENCE

husband for standing up for their beliefs. How could her older brother still be giving her orders?

"I'm not throwing you out, Julia," her brother said coldly. "I'm asking you to leave."

"I see little difference between asking me to leave and ordering it," Julia said bitterly. "And what is your reason? That Alexander and I are Patriots and you are a Loyalist?"

"Don't you see that it goes deeper than that?" Jordan asked. "We have always had our differences. But now there is a real war going on. And you and I are on opposite sides."

Julia had not thought of it that way before. She knew Jordan was right. In the past, their arguments had been battles of words. But now Julia and her husband were fighting for the Patriot cause against the British. And Jordan still insisted he would be a loyal British subject. The brother and sister had become enemies.

A gloomy silence fell over the room. Not wishing to end their discussion yet, Jordan set out steaming bowls of porridge, and Julia joined him at the table.

"You will have to forgive my table manners," Julia said. "I have not eaten since I left my home in Rhode Island."

"There is cornbread in the cupboard," Jordan said. "And I will have tea ready in a moment." He swung the iron kettle over the fire. These were the first friendly words between them in many months.

As they ate, Julia thought back over the ending of their friendship. Their arguments had started nearly two years ago. The first one had been over the Boston Tea Party. Julia had cheered the news that Patriots, dressed like Native Americans, had dumped British tea in Boston Harbor. It showed the hatred Patriots had for the tea tax. But Jordan had insisted that the Sons of Liberty were nothing but criminals. "They should be put in irons," he had said.

The brother and sister drifted farther apart as troubles between America and Great Britain grew worse.

King George and Parliament were determined to make the colonies submit to their rule. The king ordered the Port of Boston closed until the tea was paid for. He sent General Thomas Gage to become a military governor. By late 1774, Boston was con-

"... You and I are on opposite sides."

trolled by the British Redcoats. Gage planned to create military rule in all of Massachusetts Colony.

The people of Boston and Massachusetts showed no signs of giving in. Patriots in every colony supported their defiant stand. Wagonloads of supplies began rolling toward Boston from as far away as South Carolina. Without their harbor to rely on, people in Boston needed the food and supplies brought by wagon. Militia units everywhere increased their training. That was when Julia's husband joined the Rhode Island militia to help Massachusetts drive the British out of Boston.

When Julia proudly announced that she had joined the Daughters of Liberty, Jordan exploded. "You call yourself a Patriot," he shouted. "But you are about to commit treason. If Father were alive, he would have your hide."

Julia had no doubts about her cause. "We have no rights if we are ruled by British bayonets," she said. "Our only chance to gain our freedom is if all the colonies work together."

After that, the brother and sister scarcely spoke. Then, in April of 1775, Alexander received word that his militia unit was heading north toward Boston. That had been almost three months ago.

As he poured the tea, Jordan asked Julia what Alexander had done.

Julia was surprised by the question. But she was also relieved to hear a calmer tone in her brother's voice. When Jordan assured her it would not stir up another fight, Julia agreed to tell her story.

Alexander's unit had gone straight north to the towns surrounding Boston. Everywhere they went, they saw that the militia were well trained and prepared. These troops called themselves the Minutemen. They were ready to fight at a moment's notice wherever the British tried to move.

Just two days before Alexander's unit arrived, the Minutemen had met a British regiment, led by General Gage, at Lexington and Concord. The Redcoats were forced to retreat to Boston. Half the British soldiers were killed or wounded trying to follow the road back to Boston.

"After that battle," Julia said, "it was a standoff. Our militia units had Gage and his soldiers pinned against Boston Harbor. But they did not have enough strength to drive them out of Boston onto their ships."

Then Gage decided to place cannons on top of the hills overlooking the city. The Americans heard about the plan. Through the night of June 15, 1775, Alexander was one of hundreds who occupied the hills. They spent the night building defenses.

"At first light," Julia continued, "the British saw

Patriot Jonathan Gardner's powder horn. Photograph courtesy of the Concord Museum, Concord, MA

what the Americans were up to. By noon, more than two thousand Redcoats were marching up Breed's Hill and Bunker Hill. Alexander said he was really frightened, Jordie. But the British kept coming at them, even though they were met with a hailstorm of bullets.

"Twice the Patriot militia drove the British back. But each time, they came on again. When every Patriot unit was out of powder and could shoot no more, they were ordered to retreat. So the Redcoats took Bunker Hill and Breed's Hill.

Julia told Jordan how the Americans had celebrated the battle even though they lost. They had proved that it was possible to beat the British. They had held their own until the powder ran out. The Patriots lost three hundred and ninety-seven soldiers. But the Redcoats paid an even heavier price for the hills, with more than one thousand killed or wounded.

Jordan was amazed by his brother-in-law's courage. As he listened, he could feel his anger toward Julia melting away. After all, Julia and Alexander were risking everything for what they believed in. Jordan was beginning to feel he should protect her, not make her leave.

"I want to apologize for what I said in anger," Jordan said.

Julia smiled. "No apology is needed. I have not

thought enough about your feelings, or Mother's. Or the memory of Father. This is a Loyalist household. It is probably better if I leave."

"If these battles lead to a declaration of war, it will force us to separate at some point," Jordan said. "But perhaps we can wait a few weeks to see which way it goes."

Julia nodded in agreement.

"No matter what happens," Jordan said, "our lives can never be the same. You are not safe where the British are in control. And Mother and I, as Loyalists, are in danger where the Patriots are in control."

Julia knew that was true. Just after Bunker Hill, she had seen some Patriots capture four men known to be Loyalists. Their bodies were covered with tar and then feathers, and they were carried around on a fence post. Then the soldiers drove the Loyalists out of town with no clothes or protection.

It was the most cruel act Julia had ever seen, and she was ashamed of the Patriots. She figured Jordan must know about such attacks.

"What do you plan to do?" Julia asked him.

"If I am certain Mother is safe, I will write to the British general and offer my services."

Julia was stunned at the thought of her brother as a Redcoat.

"If we are in danger here," Jordan added, "we will join the thousands of Loyalists moving to Canada."

Julia shook her head. There was no way out.

The family was divided for good, or at least for many years.

Jordan stood up and clapped his hand on Julia's shoulder. "We still have some time together as brother and sister," he said quietly.

STORY NOTES

Before the American Revolution, about 10 to 20 percent of all Americans supported the British. Approximately 60,000 Loyalists like Jordan joined the British cause. Another 100,000 left their homes and fled to England or Canada. Thousands more kept their feelings to themselves and stayed where they were. Julia and Jordan's story is fictional, but many colonial families found themselves divided between Patriots and Loyalists.

There were also divided loyalties among Native Americans. The Iroquois, Shawnee, Delaware, and Cherokee fought with the British in hopes of ridding themselves of the colonists. A smaller number of Native Americans fought alongside the colonists.

African Americans were also divided. The British offered freedom to slaves who joined their armies. Many slaves accepted the British offer. The colonists, however, did not allow slaves or free blacks to join the Continental Army until war was declared. Eventually, about 5,000 African Americans fought in the Colonial Army or Navy— some earning their freedom. In 1781, about one fourth of the soldiers with Washington were African Americans.

Word Study

Here is a list of words that were commonly used around the time of the American Revolution. Write the correct word in each sentence.

cobblestones   hearth   Minutemen   treason

sconce   porridge   defiant   irons

1. The old street was paved with _____.

2. The candle in the _____ gave light to the room.

3. They placed the prisoners in shackles or_____.

4. The spy was captured and charged with the crime of _____.

5. The hungry men ate bowls of hot _____.

6. Although they were warned about the dangers, the colonists remained _____ of British laws.

7. The man lit a fire in the _____ and started to cook breakfast.

8. The militia became known as _____ because they were ready to fight at a moment's notice.

Story Facts and Ideas

Jordan Sherwood was a Loyalist. His sister Julia was a Patriot. The quotations below show different points of view. Write *Loyalist* in front of the quotations that Jordan might have said. Write *Patriot* in front of those that Julia might have said. Then, for the last two items, write something you think Julia might have said and something Jordan might have said.

_____ 1. "I feel like joining the militia and fighting those Redcoats."

_____ 2. "We are loyal British subjects and must remain loyal to the king."

_____ 3. "You call yourself a Patriot. I call you a criminal."

_____ 4. "We have no rights if we are ruled by British bayonets."

_____ 5. "Our only chance to gain our freedom is to fight."

_____ 6. "I will write General Gage and offer my services to the British army."

_____ 7.

_____ 8.

Questions to Talk and Write About

1. What would a Patriot say about a Loyalist?

2. Why was Jordan so angry when Julia joined the Daughters of Liberty?

3. Describe what the British did to punish the colonies after the Boston Tea Party. What effect did this have on the American colonies?

4. The British won the Battle of Bunker Hill. But the Patriots felt that they were winners, too. Why?

5. What did Jordan mean when he said, "No matter what happens, our lives can never be the same"?

Things to Do

1. This story ends just as the American Revolution begins. Tell what might have happened to Jordan and Julia twenty years later. Did the family get back together? Or did Jordan and Julia go their separate ways?

2. Imagine that you are Julia. Write a letter that she might have written to her mother. Tell how you feel about being sent away from your home by your brother. Explain why you feel the way you do about fighting the British.

4. Act out the scene from the story between Jordan and Julia.

5. Carefully reread what Jordan thinks about fighting the British. Then prepare a speech or write a newspaper editorial expressing the Loyalist view.

"Give Me Liberty, or Give Me Death!"

The period of the American Revolution was a time of bold actions, brave leadership, and inspiring words. Those inspiring words were sometimes in writing, like the Declaration of Independence. Other words that helped move Americans to declare independence were in speeches. Some, like this speech by Patrick Henry in 1775, are still well known today.

Here is what Patrick Henry said to his fellow citizens in Virginia to draw Americans into united action:

> "Gentlemen may cry, peace, peace—but there is no peace. The war is actually begun! The next gale that sweeps from the north will bring to our ears the clash of resounding arms! Our brethren, in Boston, are already in the field! Why stand we here idle? . . . Is life so dear, or peace so sweet, as to be purchased at the price of chains and slavery? Forbid it, Almighty God! I know not what course others may take; but as for me, give me liberty, or give me death!"

A Time for Courage

In what ways did John and Abigail Adams show courage in 1776?

Background

John Adams was a revolutionary leader in Boston. At the time of this story, the problems between the colonies and Britain were growing. When he was elected to the Continental Congress in 1774, John went to Philadelphia. He and the other delegates were deciding what to do about the British. Many tried to find ways to reach a compromise with Britain.

John's wife Abigail was also a Patriot. While John was away, Abigail took over all the responsibilities of managing their farm and business affairs as well as taking care of their four children.

For the next ten years, John's work with the Congress kept him away from home most of the time. During this time, John and Abigail wrote frequent letters to each other.

This story contains some of the things that John and Abigail wrote to each other. All the letters are based on fact. The letters begin just a few months before the start of the American Revolution. The colonists had not yet declared their independence, but the fighting had started.

AMERICA'S WAR FOR INDEPENDENCE

Braintree, Mass.
March 16, 1776

My Dear Husband,

Last evening I received your letter of March 8. A pleasant surprise to receive a letter from Philadelphia in only seven days.

This late evening hour is my special time to write to you. Your four Favorites are all asleep and the house is still.

After our bitter winter, the weather has turned mild and sunny. I am hoping for good crops this year. Better than last, although the English corn [wheat] was excellent. I bought a parcel of timberland and have hired help for the spring planting as well as the dairy. I hope in some time to have the reputation of being as good a farmer as you have been a good statesman.

I sense that something important is about to happen. For more than a week we have been watching British ships arrive. They anchor outside Boston Harbor so they are in full view. Ezra says he has counted eighty-two ships.

What are the British up to? Everyone here believes they are about to leave Boston. For two years they have held that town captive, turning it into a fortress. Now, all our neighbors say, they are pulling out.

I pray that it is true. I shall hasten to find out more before I close this letter.

Sunday, Noon

Almost as soon as I was asleep last night, I was awakened by a cannonade. The thundering sound came, of course, from Boston. It continued from midnight until nine this morning. It was impossible to sleep.

I have now learned the cause of all those cannon volleys. General Washington's troops seized Bunker and Breed's hills overlooking Boston. They placed their cannons there, pointing straight down at the British. Realizing that they could not defend themselves from attack, the British troops were loaded aboard their ships. They are quitting Boston.

I shall not breathe easy until they are under sail.

My dear friend, I wish you were here with me. All our friends are elated, but I am worried. It appears that we are in for a long war. The British will now invade some other place, perhaps less prepared to fight back than Boston. Every foot of ground the British take now, we must make them fight for. And let us make them pay the same price that Bunker Hill cost them.

Abigail Adams. Painting by Gilbert Stuart.

AMERICA'S WAR FOR INDEPENDENCE

Monday morning

An officer serving with General Washington is on his way to Philadelphia. He has kindly offered to deliver my letter directly to your hand. I have but minutes to complete my thoughts.

I am proud of you, my dear husband, for all the work you have done for Congress and our country. And I think that one of your wisest decisions, my husband, was to nominate General Washington as commander in chief. When I met him, I was even more impressed than you had prepared me to be. He is a noble and commanding figure.

At first I was worried about him since he is a Virginian. I have doubts about what Virginians and other representatives from slaveholding states mean when they talk about liberty. As you know, I think that slavery is a terrible evil and should be abolished. It has a terrible effect on character and society. I believe in the equality of rights for all people.

Washington, however, seems to be a good man, and his presence shows the British that all the Colonies are united in their desire to be free. The Continental Army he created here from militia units made us all proud. We also felt safer. Now he has succeeded in forcing the British from Boston.

Today I find that I am indeed amazed by that event. We have retaken Boston from the British, and not one drop of blood has been shed.

The messenger is here and I must bid you farewell. The children all send their love to Papa.

Yours,

Abigail

Story Facts and Ideas I

Answer these questions about the preceding letter with complete sentences.

1. How did Abigail help make it possible for John to attend the Congress?

2. Why was she worried even after the British left Boston?

3. What did Abigail mean when she wrote, "Make the British pay the same price that Bunker Hill cost them"?

4. What did Abigail think about the appointment of George Washington when she first heard the news?

*Philadelphia
April 10, 1776*

𝒟*earest Abigail,*

The news from Boston has filled us with hope here. Several friends in Congress have had the pleasure of reading your three recent letters. They agree with the wisdom of your concerns about what the British may do next. Many feel that Virginia will next face invasion. General Washington, however, believes New York will be their target. I fear we shall soon find out.

Words cannot express my pride in you and our townspeople in this past year of trials. You, in particular, my dear Abigail, are a constant source of amazement. I do believe my friends wonder at my good fortune in having such a companion.

This afternoon I took a stroll through the pleasant garden behind my lodging. In this rare moment of quiet, I reflected on all you have done and endured.

It is now just short of a year since the fighting began at Lexington and Concord. During all that time, you have lived with the danger of British attack. Here in the safety of Philadelphia, I can only imagine what you have been through.

Through all of this, you raise our daughter and three sons and must see to their education. You have managed the Farm with great skill. Somehow you taught yourself to be a farmer in only two seasons. You have kept my law office in order and managed the finances. I had thought my long months at Congress would put us heavily in debt. You have avoided that.

Often I am troubled by not being there to help you. I felt helpless when I heard that an epidemic of dysentery had swept through Boston and many were dying. But I did not even know that you and all the children had been stricken. By the time the

John Adams. Painting by Charles Willson Peale. Courtesy Independence National Park

mail came to me, six weeks had passed. All of you but Patsy were fully recovered before I even knew of your plight.

Now, at least, the British menace has been removed. I hope that this will lighten your cares. Remember, though, my dearest friend, that this is a time for the greatest courage. You and I have already sacrificed three years of our life together. We must both be prepared for these separations to last many more months.

Later this day

You have often asked when Congress will take up the matter of Independence. I can tell you now we are about to decide the greatest issue in the history of America. The time is right. I believe the Congress is ready to sever all ties with Great Britain.

As you know, I have been impatient for this moment since the war began. I was annoyed by the caution of my fellow delegates. And I was angry when they wrote one final petition to King George. Look what happened! The King would not even read it.

Now I believe the delay has been a blessing. There has been time for the people of every Colony to debate the issue. In this way, the doubts have slowly been removed. Now when we act, all the people will act together—except for a few stubborn Loyalists.

I hope to be able to send you the great news before long. Meantime, write as often as you can.

Fondly,

John

Story Facts and Ideas II

Answer these questions about the preceding letter in complete sentences.

1. What did John say he admired about his wife?

2. What did John say about independence?

Boston
July 14, 1776

My Dear Husband,

I have before me your letters of July 3 and 4. Your letters always give me pleasure. But these are even more welcome, for they deal with the future happiness of our Country.

I am very happy and gratified that my husband has been a major actor in this great drama. In my mind, I can picture the serious deliberations of your Committee. I can see you and the other members carefully working on the document that was written by Mr. Jefferson.

We went to King Street for the proclamation. Colonel Craft read the Declaration of Independence from the balcony of the State House. A great crowd was there and they listened with care to every word.

When the Colonel finished, the cry from the balcony was, "God save our American States!" The crowd raised three mighty cheers. Then cannons were fired from the ships and the troops raised their rifles and fired into the air. Every bell in the town rang in celebration. I have never seen more joyful faces.

I had dinner with Colonel and Mrs. Craft and many friends who send you congratulations. Everywhere people are following the advice of Congress to create new state governments. Their days as colonies are over. Government now will be based on the will of the people, not on the power of a King.

In every state, too, we hear that all signs of royal authority have been removed. A man named Mr. Farley read us a report from New York. There, when the Declaration was read, General Washington's troops joined the celebration. They pulled down a statue of King George on horse-back. The lead from this statue is to be melted down and run into bullets for the army.

After dinner, we went back out in King Street. There, people had gathered the King's arms and other objects from the State House. A great bonfire was lit, marking the end of royal authority in this state.

Even in this moment of joy we all know the future will not be easy. Years of struggle will be needed to preserve this Independence. And I know

also that the sacrifice you and I make must continue. Therefore, always add a few lines to tell me about yourself and your Health. It is important for the children to hear that you are well.

Ever yours,

Abigail

Story Facts and Ideas III

1. What did Abigail mean when she called her husband "a major actor in a great drama"?

2. What happened in Boston after Colonel Craft read the Declaration of Independence?

3. Why did John and Abigail believe that they would still have to make sacrifices after independence had been won?

AMERICA'S WAR FOR INDEPENDENCE

Independence Hall, Pennsylvania, meeting place of the Continental Congress.

STORY NOTES

John and Abigail Adams were both quite amazing in their own way. The new nation sent John on many important missions to Europe. All together, John and Abigail were kept apart by the nation's needs for 17 years. In 1796, John Adams was elected the second president of the United States. He and Abigail would be the first to occupy the newly built White House.

As for Abigail, she was known as quite an independent thinker. She spoke strongly in favor of the colonies declaring their independence many years before most thought it possible. And in her letters to John, she frequently expressed her displeasure with the differences she saw in the education of girls and boys—as well as laws that prohibited African Americans from attending school. Throughout her life, she was an outspoken believer in equal rights.

Word Study

Circle the word or phrase that has almost the same meaning as the underlined word in each sentence. Then write sentences using each of the underlined words.

1. Abigail was awakened by the noise of the cannonade.

   sweet drink   loud sound of firing cannons   fast moves

2. The committee had serious deliberations about the Declaration of Independence.

   discussions   deliveries   insects

3. The Patriots were elated when they heard that the British were leaving Boston.

   depressed   hungry   happy

4. An epidemic raced through Boston, and many people became ill.

   horseman   noise   sickness

5. Abigail was gratified that her husband was a hero.

   pleased   angry   lonely

6. When Abigail received a letter, she would hasten to answer.

   delay   hurry   shout

7. John walked in the garden behind his lodging.

   house   farm   ship

8. The British were a menace to Boston.

   threat   friend   traitor

9. Congress decided to sever ties with England.

   increase   cut   work

AMERICA'S WAR FOR INDEPENDENCE

Questions to Talk and Write About

1. Explain why Abigail was both worried and happy when the British left Boston.

2. Why was John Adams at first impatient about how long it took Congress to decide on independence? Why did he later think the delay was good?

3. Describe Abigail Adams. Make a list of the things she did while John was gone. Tell what qualities helped her succeed.

4. John and Abigail Adams did not fight the British on the battlefield. Yet they were both very important to the American Revolution. What special kind of courage did they have?

5. Explain why the American people still needed great courage after the Declaration of Independence.

Things to Do

1. Pretend that you are one of the Adams children. Write a letter to your father telling him what your life is like and what you think about his work.

2. Use a reference book to learn more about John and Abigail Adams. Make a list of 20 facts about these famous Americans.

3. Carefully read the Declaration of Independence in a history text or other reference book. Some of the language may be difficult to understand, so you may need to work with a partner.

4. Imagine that you were in Boston when the Declaration of Independence was read. Write an entry in your journal describing the scene.

5. When the United States declared its independence, it needed a flag. Use library books to find pictures of early American flags. Design a flag that you might have made at that time.

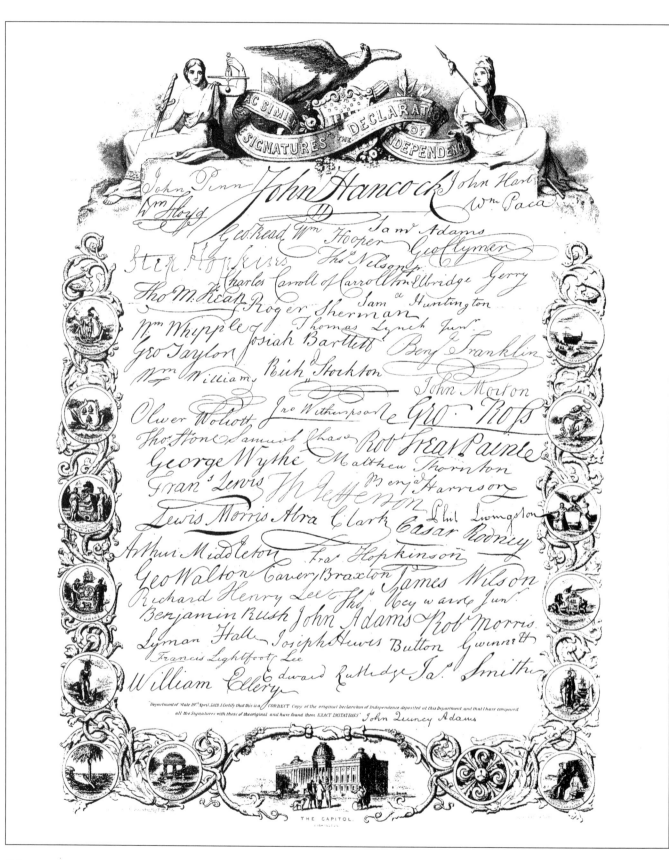

AMERICA'S WAR FOR INDEPENDENCE

Washington's Shadow Army

What qualities made George Washington a great military leader?

Background

When the British were driven from Boston in the spring of 1776, they sailed to Canada. A few months later, they invaded Long Island and Staten Island, near New York City. General George Washington had guessed that New York was where the British would strike. Washington had already moved his Continental Army to New York and had put up defenses.

However, the British Army that attacked New York numbered nearly thirty-two thousand soldiers and was very well equipped. Washington and his army fought skillfully but were greatly outnumbered and had to flee New York, leaving it to the British.

This is where we pick up our story. The story is in the form of a journal kept by a fictional character named Captain Nathaniel Harper. The events he describes are based on fact.

The Journal of Captain Nathaniel Harper

Camp in eastern Pennsylvania, December 21, 1776

For several weeks now, we have been in a zigzag retreat across New Jersey. The two British generals, Howe and Cornwallis, have been chasing us. They line up in straight rows and fire—just as they do in Europe. They keep trying to trap us in an open battle. Whenever we are in trouble, we fall back into the woods and reappear when they don't expect it.

General Washington knows how badly we are outnumbered. Time and again, we have slipped from the grasp of the British just as they prepared to do battle.

Washington used the same tactic when we fled New York. The British had us trapped, and their fleet covered all the escape routes. But the General used the cover of fog and darkness to guide us across the Hudson River in small boats. When the Redcoats attacked in the morning, they found us gone.

I am an aide to General Washington and work closely with him every day. He has often explained his strategy to me and to other officers.

"We cannot risk a total defeat," he tells us. "We must always keep the Continental Army in the field. That is a message to Great Britain and the world that our War for Independence goes on."

Once we crossed the Delaware River into Pennsylvania, the British gave up the chase. This has given us some time to rest. Some of the wives who have followed their husbands into the battlefield are nursing the sick and trying to mend our uniforms.

I suspect that it would surprise some people if they realized that more than a few women marched with us—some with their children. The British Army, I hear, has also hired women to cook and help care for the sick.

We are all weary, and it is good to hear that General Howe has returned to New York for the winter.

Earlier this evening, I met with Washington in his headquarters. In the lantern light, I could see several maps spread on his table. He asked me about the spirits of the troops. I told him that they were discouraged and that many had left to go home. The loss at New York and the endless retreats have worn them down.

He nodded solemnly. "And as their duty time ends," he added, "many have said that they will not reenlist. We have one third the troops we had at Boston."

Then he asked me a startling question. "Do you think a mid-winter victory will improve their mood?"

He laughed at my puzzled look as he pointed at a map. "We are going to re-cross the Delaware and strike the British garrison here at Trenton. Tell the officers to get their men ready. At dawn, take some men and ride ahead to round up as many boats as you can."

"Trenton is held by Hessians," he continued. "They will be even less on their guard than the British." Hessians are the German troops hired by King George. The men hate these mercenaries because they are soldiers that fight only for money. They do not fight for any cause.

I asked him when we would attack. He answered with just a hint of a smile, "On Christmas night."

AMERICA'S WAR FOR INDEPENDENCE

January 10, 1777
Morristown, New Jersey

On Christmas night 1776, we crossed the Delaware River. The weather was terrible, and the river was clogged with ice. Rain had turned to snow, and the wind blew like a hurricane.

My boat was the first to reach the New Jersey shore. I ordered the men to build fires. We were soaking wet and freezing cold. Worse than that, the powder was hopelessly wet. I feared that not a single rifle would fire.

It was dawn before we reached the Hessian stronghold. By good fortune, the Germans had slept late after celebrating Christmas.

General Washington instructed me to pass the order, "Charge bayonets and rush on!" He knew that only about one man in five had a bayonet. But he also knew that our rifles would not discharge.

We entered the fort before the Hessians knew we were there. They managed only a few harmless pistol shots before they ran out or surrendered.

That short Battle of Trenton was an outstanding victory. No Americans were killed, and we captured the entire Hessian brigade—nine hundred men, plus one thousand rifles and six valuable brass cannons.

A week later, we met the largest British force in New Jersey at Princeton. The Redcoats broke through our lines. It looked like our men would bolt and run. But Washington refused to retreat. He was a marvel to watch. Our troops gathered around him. Within minutes the Redcoats were on the run.

One of the British prisoners said to me, "Your General Washington is a genius. His army is nowhere and then it is everywhere. For us, it has been like fighting a shadow."

March 21, 1778
Valley Forge, Pennsylvania

More than a year has passed since I have written in this journal. It has been a year of defeats and retreating. We have seen our Army shrink to a few hundred ragged soldiers. We tried to survive the winter in our camp at Valley Forge.

I have waited for a time of hope to start writing again. Now, as the spring of 1778 blooms, that time has come.

Our worst defeat in 1777 came when General Howe captured Philadelphia. It was a surprise move. He sailed up the Chesapeake Bay with an army of twenty thousand. Washington led us in one battle to hold them back but failed.

Howe took over Philadelphia, forcing the members of our Congress to flee to Lancaster. Howe decided to winter in at Philadelphia. He paid no attention to our pitiful camp at Valley Forge a few miles away.

It is hard for me to write about those winter months. From the start, we were short of food. Our Thanksgiving dinner was rice with vinegar. Few men had uniforms any longer. They wore what they received from home or from the Daughters of Liberty.

Many of the men and women went through the winter without boots. They wrapped their feet in rags. We had few coats or cloaks. We lost many lives to cold, illness, and hunger.

Even Washington's hopes grew dim. One evening he said to me, "I think ten more days will finish us, Nat." Then an idea came to him.

The next day, Washington put a volunteer from Germany named Friedrich von Steuben in charge. He was an experienced soldier and taught us to drill and use bayonets like his troops in Germany. The training took our minds off our troubles and

made us more disciplined soldiers. Another foreign volunteer taught us artillery.

As spring approached, fresh food and supplies reached us. With that and our hard training, we were ready to fight.

Yesterday some members of Congress visited our camp. They praised us for keeping American hopes alive. One man told us that newspapers in Great Britain and other European countries said that Washington was one of the great generals of history. Everyone knew of our struggle.

I think Washington was glad to hear that Congress had confidence in him. He had lost more battles than he had won. Any other general would have been replaced.

Now we are waiting for new weapons and new troops. We have learned that the British are quitting Philadelphia. Howe is to be replaced for failing to defeat us. The scales have now tipped in our favor.

STORY NOTES

Of the 11,000 soldiers at Valley Forge during the winter of 1777–1778, Washington said that almost 3,000 were unfit to fight because they did not have shoes or proper clothing. Toward the end of the war, Washington became enraged when it was suggested that he used the army to have himself crowned king. By many, he was already considered a national hero.

Valley Forge

AMERICA'S WAR FOR INDEPENDENCE

Word Study

Read the three words in each row. Cross out the word that does not belong with the others. Then tell why that word does not belong.

1. tactic   strategy   discipline   _____

2. Cornwallis   mercenaries   Hessians   _____

3. aide   brigade   helper   _____

4. prey   victim   garrison   _____

5. bolts   feats   deeds   _____

6. Washington   Cornwallis   Howe   _____

Story Facts and Ideas

In a sentence or two for each item, tell how . . .

1. Washington led his army in their escape from the British in New York.

2. women took part in Washington's army.

3. Washington commanded his troops at the Battle of Princeton.

4. the officers helped the soldiers keep their spirits high at Valley Forge.

5. Washington won such a great reputation as a general.

Questions to Talk and Write About

1. Why didn't General Washington want his army to fight a big open battle with the British? Why didn't the British generals force Washington to fight them in the open?

2. Why does the author call Washington's forces "a shadow army"?

3. The Continental Army spent a hard winter at Valley Forge. What problems made the winter difficult? How was the army improved because of that winter?

4. The British had a powerful army. They captured the two largest cities in America, New York and Philadelphia. Why didn't they easily defeat the Americans?

5. Make a list of the qualities that made General Washington a great leader. Using this list, write a paragraph describing George Washington.

Things to Do

1. Imagine you are a soldier in the Continental Army. Write a letter home about one of the battles from this story or about your winter at Valley Forge.

2. Men were leaving Washington's army in great numbers. Prepare a short speech that you might use to convince them to stay.

3. Friedrich von Steuben, a foreign volunteer who helped Washington, is mentioned in this story. Another hero was Marquis de Lafayette from France. Use library books to find out more about these heroes. Prepare a brief report on one of them.

AMERICA'S WAR FOR INDEPENDENCE

The Turning Point

What made a single battle the turning point in the American Revolution?

In a house just outside Paris, Benjamin Franklin was working on a report to Congress. The fall weather was still warm, so the glass doors of his study were open. Outside, he could hear dry leaves rattling across the garden path.

This fall of 1777 marked two years that Franklin had been living in France. Congress had sent Franklin to France on a special mission. He was to try to convince the French to join the American side in the war against England. Without France's help, Congress was not sure they could defeat the mighty British.

Franklin finished the report, blotted it, and wiped his quill. He wished he had better news to send to his friends in Congress. But, as in all his reports, he could tell of no progress. So far, there was no sign that France would become America's ally.

Franklin stepped out into the garden. His mind drifted back to his first meeting with Count de Vergennes. Vergennes, the foreign minister for King Louis XVI, was a brilliant man who soon became a good friend. He was the official Franklin met with most often.

AMERICA'S WAR FOR INDEPENDENCE

Benjamin Franklin

When they first met in 1775, Franklin knew that Vergennes favored the American cause. Like everyone in France, he was pleased to see the British having trouble. He had even secretly arranged to send shiploads of weapons and supplies to the Patriots. He had convinced Spain to do the same. Those supplies had helped to equip Washington's Continental Army.

In their meeting, Vergennes made it clear to Franklin that he would not do anything more. "I will be blunt with you, Dr. Franklin," he had said. "Only a dozen years ago we were at war with Great Britain for seven costly years. We lost much of our empire to them. Our young king does not want to risk another humiliating defeat. And you are asking us to take that risk."

Franklin thought for a moment, then answered, "We are certain we can win this war. But it may take many years. We seek French help in order to hasten our victory and our independence."

Vergennes smiled. "Prove to me that America can win. Come to me with news that you have beaten the British in a major battle. Then we will reconsider."

In the long months since then, Franklin continued to work and hope. He carefully studied the contents of every mail pouch from America. But there was no sign of that major victory Vergennes asked for.

During those two years, Congress sometimes sent other Americans to help Franklin. They quickly grew impatient. No matter how many meetings were held, the French officials would not change their minds.

Franklin made the most of the long months of waiting, enjoying the splendor of Paris. His arrival in France had been treated as a great social event. Everyone was eager to meet the most famous of all Americans. Lords and ladies in the Court of Louis XVI invited him to every banquet and ball. Leaders in business, government, and science made him the guest of honor at dinners, concerts, and other occasions. The little appointment book Franklin carried was always filled with invitations.

At these social events, a crowd would gather around him. In his fur cap and plain suit, Franklin stood out among the powdered wigs and elegant clothes of the French men and women. He enjoyed the attention. Throughout Europe he was famous as a writer, an inventor, a scientist, a thinker, and a Patriot leader.

Often people wanted to hear the story of his early beginnings. They listened with fascination as he told of starting work when he was twelve. He had been a printer's apprentice for his older brother in Boston. When he was seventeen, Franklin had struck out on his own. He loved to tell about arriving in Philadelphia with only a few coins in his pocket.

He had worked hard and saved his money. Soon he had his own printing company. He became a publisher, producing a weekly magazine called the *Saturday Evening Post.* He wrote and published *Poor Richard's Almanack*. The *Almanack* had useful information about farming and business. But it made him famous because it was filled with his wise and witty sayings. Those sayings, such as "the early bird gets the worm," became known throughout the colonies and Europe.

Franklin knew his French friends liked stories of adventure and success in the American colonies. Though the colonies now had cities and more than one and a half million people, the French still thought of the colonies as places where rugged pioneers lived a frontier life. To them the colonies were a land of opportunity where a person could start with nothing and rise to a position of wealth and fame.

Franklin seemed like the perfect American success story. He had not only gained wealth and fame

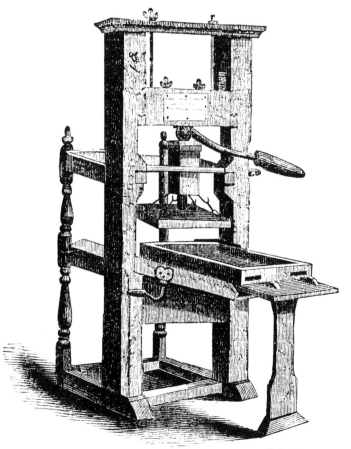

Printing press

but was also considered one of the world's great scientists. Franklin would often tell his French friends that wealth was important for only one reason: It gave him time to do all the other things he was interested in. It gave him time to invent such useful things as the Franklin stove, the lightning rod, and bifocal glasses. It also gave him time for his experiments with electricity.

Franklin was a fascinating man and a great storyteller. At social gatherings, people wanted to know about his life in Philadelphia. How had he gained the support to bring America the first hospital, the first public library, and the first insurance company? How had he made Philadelphia the first American city with street lighting, a police department, and a fire company?

Of all his achievements, Franklin liked most to discuss his work for America itself. He had helped write the Declaration of Independence, and he had been the first to offer a plan for a unified government. He had organized the first postal system. And when the trouble with Great Britain began, Franklin had worked hard for the Continental Congress.

Now in his seventies, Franklin had as much energy as ever. He was enjoying the dazzling social life of Paris. And he liked being the center of attention. But he hoped he could use his popularity for the sake of his fellow Americans. He wanted to complete his mission.

When he had finished his walk in the garden, Franklin returned to his study. A messenger was waiting for him. He had a note from Vergennes, asking Franklin to meet him.

Within minutes, Franklin was in his carriage, clattering through the crowded streets. He had always loved the view of towering cathedrals and the graceful Seine River. But on this trip he was more concerned about why Vergennes had sent for him. He must have some news.

Vergennes was in his office studying a large

map of North America on the wall. The foreign minister greeted Franklin and drew him closer to the map. Vergennes said that he did have news, hinting that it came from a spy in Canada.

"I think our major battle may be taking shape," Vergennes said. "But I am afraid it does not look hopeful for your countrymen."

With a long pointer, he touched key spots on the map as he talked. "The British plan to divide the country at the Hudson River," he said. "General

> # For the first time, the waiting filled him with anxiety and worry.

Burgoyne will move south from Canada with four thousand British soldiers, three thousand Hessians, and fourteen hundred Native American troops. General Howe will march north from Philadelphia. A third army, with Iroquois allies, will come across New York from the west. When these armies meet, then snip—New England will be cut off."

He moved his fingers like a pair of scissors cutting straight up the Hudson River. Franklin did not like the looks of it. But he dared not show any signs of doubt. He peered at the map through his bifocals.

Franklin turned to Vergennes. "General Howe may move north," he said in a confident voice, "but the militia will rise up as it did at Boston. Burgoyne will have trouble moving south. The British must carry their supplies from Lake Champlain to the Hudson. Picture them loaded with supplies, tracking through heavy forest. Our militia will give them much to think about."

Vergennes smiled, admiring Franklin's confidence. "I hope that you are right, Doctor. The future of your country may be at stake."

Franklin returned to his house, and weeks of uncertainty followed. For the first time, the waiting filled him with anxiety and worry. By now the battle had been fought, but news was painfully slow. Usually letters from America took four or five weeks to reach him. Sometimes the merchant ship carrying the mail was captured by the British. There was always a chance that a report of the battle had been sent but was now in British hands.

Finally the mail pouch he had been waiting for arrived. Inside were several reports, including one from General Washington. A battle had been fought at Saratoga, near Albany, and the British had surrendered to American troops under the command of General Horatio Gates. The Americans had won. Franklin picked up his fur hat and joyfully threw it across the room. Finally he could tell Vergennes of a major victory.

At the Ministry, Vergennes greeted him warmly. He, too, had received news of the battle but knew no details. Franklin was delighted to supply those details. He had read through the report on his ride to the Ministry.

Franklin explained that Howe never moved from Philadelphia. No one knew why. The force that came east along the Mohawk River was defeated by the New York militia. The main British army under Burgoyne ran into the trouble that Franklin had guessed.

"When he was near Albany," Franklin said, "Burgoyne ran into the Continental Army. With the Continentals' artillery and with militia swarming all over him, Burgoyne surrendered at Saratoga to General Horatio Gates."

Franklin handed him the brief report from Washington. That report removed any doubt about the accuracy of the news.

"Amazing," Vergennes said as he finished the

report. "Gentleman Jack Burgoyne has suffered a defeat that will end his career. Look at this, my friend: Five thousand Redcoats surrendered. Three hundred officers and five generals. A most impressive victory. You must be very proud."

"Indeed I am," Franklin answered. "I know that *Poor Richard*'s must contain a saying I might use. But in the excitement of this moment I cannot recall a single one."

Vergennes laughed. "You will have time to quote more of your sayings to me. Right now we must think of the work at hand. We must get our troops and ships in action before you Americans end the war without us."

On the ride back to his house, Ben Franklin breathed a sigh of relief. Finally, after twenty-seven months, he had completed his mission for America.

STORY NOTES

Following the American victory at Saratoga, the French signed a treaty and became active in the American Revolution. They sent approximately 12,000 soldiers and 32,000 sailors to help General George Washington. Franklin wanted to return to Philadelphia but was asked to stay on for another two years. While in Paris, Franklin worked with John Adams and John Jay on all negotiations with the French.

The events in this story are true. The conversations, however, were made up to give you a sense of what might have been said.

Franklin returned to America in 1785 and was a member of the Constitutional Convention. He lived to be 84. His daughter Sarah organized a Daughters of Liberty chapter that made clothing and sent shipments of medical supplies to the Continental Army.

Word Study

Below are descriptions of things that helped make Benjamin Franklin famous as an inventor and as a writer. Write the name of the invention after the description. Then list two more inventions or ideas that made Franklin famous. You may need to do some research to find some of the answers.

1. eyeglasses with a two-part lens, one part for seeing things up close and one part for objects far away

2. a book of information and witty sayings

3. an iron stove shaped like a fireplace

4. a metal pole that attracts lightning and directs it into the ground

5. a weekly magazine that Franklin published

6.

7.

Story Facts and Ideas

This paragraph has ten sentences. Five of the sentences are true; five are not. Cross out the five false statements. Then, on another sheet of paper, rewrite the paragraph, making all the facts true.

(1) Benjamin Franklin was a great soldier who fought next to George Washington on the battlefield. (2) Congress sent Franklin to Paris to get the French to join the war against England. (3) Franklin became a popular person in Paris and loved living there. (4) But the French king wouldn't join the war because he didn't think the Americans needed any help. (5) Franklin met often with Vergennes, the French foreign minister, who was his friend. (6) Vergennes told Franklin about a British plan to defeat the Americans. (7) Franklin was afraid and told Vergennes that the British plan would probably work. (8) Franklin waited nervously for news of the battle. (9) The news arrived; the British had won a major victory. (10) "Now," said Vergennes, "we will join your war, because we know you are weak. We know you need our help."

AMERICA'S WAR FOR INDEPENDENCE

Questions to Talk and Write About

1. Why do you think Congress felt that Ben Franklin was the best person to send to France?

2. Tell how Franklin described life in America. Why did the French people enjoy his accounts? How was life in the New World different from life in Europe?

3. Why did the French want to become involved in the American Revolution?

4. Make a list of words that could be used to describe what type of person Benjamin Franklin was. Then write a short description using the words on your list.

5. The Battle of Saratoga is called the most important battle of the American Revolution. Why does the author of the story call this "The Turning Point"?

Things to Do

1. Do more research on Benjamin Franklin. Prepare a brief report on the part he played in the Continental Congress, his activities in Paris, or some of his inventions. Explain how he helped improve life for people in America.

2. Using reference books from the library, explore the role that France played in the American Revolution.

3. On the map that follows, draw the lines to show what Vergennes explained to Franklin about the British battle plan.

4. Act out the two meetings between Franklin and Vergennes in the story. Scene I is their first meeting in 1775. Scene 2 is the meeting about the American victory at Saratoga. Use lines from the story or invent other conversation that you think fits.

5. Write a story about Benjamin Franklin that might have appeared in a Paris newspaper.

Reading a Battle Map

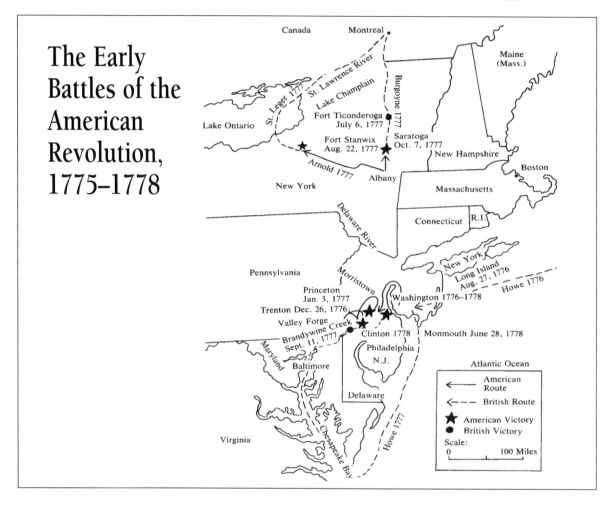

The Early Battles of the American Revolution, 1775–1778

This map shows the major battles during the first two years of the Revolutionary War. It also shows the lines of march and the water routes taken by the different armies. Use the map to answer these questions.

1. Who attacked New York by sea? While Washington zigzagged through New Jersey, what did General Howe do?

2. The Americans fought the British in two smaller battles in 1777 before defeating them at Saratoga. What were those two smaller battles?

3. How far is Valley Forge from Philadelphia?

4. During the two years of war, which side traveled the greatest distance on land? Which side won more battles? Can you think of reasons why it was harder for the British to fight?

48

America's Story

The Martin Women

How did the Martin women help the American Revolution in the South?

Background

After their loss at the Battle of Saratoga, the British decided to invade the Southern states where they believed they would get more help from local Loyalists than they had in the North. If they won the South, the British were sure they could destroy the revolutionary hopes of the Patriots once and for all. Most of the remaining battles of the American Revolution would now be fought in the Southern colonies.

The story about the Martin women is true.

There was no quiver in her voice. There were no tears in her eyes. Elizabeth Marshall Martin looked with pride at her seven oldest sons. How she wished their father were still alive and could see them now. At last, she spoke quietly but with great feeling. "Go with my blessing. Join the Continental Army. Do all you can for your country." Then she added, "If I were a man, I'd go with you."

"I can't help worrying about leaving you out here, mother," said the eldest son. "How will you take care of the farm and the younger children all by yourself?"

"Don't worry. I'll manage," she replied. "Besides, Grace and Rachel have volunteered to stay with me."

Grace and Rachel were Mrs. Martin's two daughters-in-law. They were tall, slim young women who were barely out of their teens. They had grown very fond of their mother-in-law. But their offer to stay went beyond fondness. They also had to be brave to live at Mrs. Martin's farm on the edge of the South Carolina wilderness. The scattered population included many Loyalists. The farm was also close to Native American territory, and the Loyalists had persuaded most of the Native Americans to join them in fighting for the British. The Loyalists were bitterly opposed to Patriots like the Martins.

After her sons left to join the Continental Army, some Loyalists began making trouble for Elizabeth Martin. Once they stormed into her house, cut open the feather beds, and scattered their contents. On another occasion, some Loyalists learned that a badly wounded Continental soldier was being cared for by the three women and demanded that he be turned over to them. When Mrs. Martin refused, a group of Loyalists burst into her home. As they searched it, they smashed furniture and her few precious items of china and pottery. They left without finding the wounded soldier hidden beneath the floorboards.

Early in 1779, the British decided that the time had come for an all-out attack on the South. They began to gather thousands of troops in the Carolinas and Georgia. Their ranks were joined by Southern Loyalists—but their numbers were far smaller than the British had hoped for. Though the Southern economy was more dependent on Britain

than was that of the North, most Southerners strongly supported the Patriot cause.

The Southern militias were no match for the British army. General George Washington ordered General Nathaniel Greene to move south to oppose the British. But his American troops were badly outnumbered. Time and again they were turned back when they tried to recapture towns such as Savannah, Georgia, and Charleston, South Carolina, from the British.

One evening during the British attack on Augusta, Georgia, the Martin women learned something startling. Late that night a courier with important messages for the British would pass on a lonely road near their home. This was their chance to serve the American cause. They felt they must act even though they would be risking their lives. They devised a plan to capture those valuable papers.

Grace and Rachel dressed in their husbands' clothes and armed themselves with rifles. They made their way cautiously to the point in the road where they knew the courier's party must pass. For several hours, they waited silently in the dark woods. They tried not to move. The crackling of twigs might give them away. They grew cold and stiff as each hour crept by.

Finally they heard the sound of horses' hoofs. They still did not move until the courier and his guards were almost in front of them. Then they leaped from the bushes and aimed their rifles at the riders. "We want that message pouch," Grace said in the deepest voice she could muster.

Completely taken by surprise, the British obeyed the command. They knew that the "men" with the rifles meant business. Then Grace and Rachel motioned for the courier and his escort to turn around and ride back in the same direction from which they had come.

As soon as the British were out of sight and hearing, Grace and Rachel spurred their horses.

AMERICA'S WAR FOR INDEPENDENCE

They raced through the woods to a secret meeting place. There they met a man who took the papers and headed for Augusta. Just an hour later, he delivered them to a grateful General Greene.

Sullenly and slowly the British courier and his guards retraced their route. When they neared the Martin farmhouse, they stopped to see if they could get something to eat. Mrs. Martin answered their impatient knocking. Pretending to be surprised to see them, she asked the travelers why they had returned so soon after passing her home earlier that evening.

"Two young rebels stopped us. They stole our papers," the courier complained.

"You mean you allowed two rebel boys to halt you? Didn't you have any guns?" Mrs. Martin asked in mock disbelief.

"Yes, we were armed. But they caught us off guard. We didn't have time to use our guns," one British soldier explained sheepishly.

"Please, come in. Be my guests," Mrs. Martin said. She was trying hard not to sound pleased. "You are welcome to rest here until morning."

The next morning, Mrs. Martin and her daughters-in-law served hot corn meal and chicory coffee to the soldiers. The Redcoats enjoyed talking to the two young women. They thanked the Martins for their hospitality and left. They still did not know that the two friendly young women were last night's rebels.

STORY NOTES

A number of women in both the North and the South served as spies and couriers during the American Revolution. Like Paul Revere, Sybil

Detail of Molly Pitcher at the Battle of Monmouth, June 28, 1778. After a painting by C.Y. Turner. The Bettmann Archive

Luddington rode across the New England countryside to warn the colonists that the British were coming. Deborah Champion of Connecticut rode on horseback for two days through British lines to carry secret reports on British troop movements to George Washington in Cambridge, Massachusetts. A Cherokee woman named Nancy Ward spied for the colonists in Tennessee. And in Charleston, South Carolina, women smuggled food out of town for hungry rebel soldiers.

A small number of women also fought during the American Revolution. Some, such as Molly Pitcher, replaced their fallen husbands on the battlefield. A few women disguised themselves as men and joined the Patriot army. One such woman was Deborah Sampson. Sampson and many of these other women were treated as heroines and were given army pensions after the war.

Word Study

A synonym is a word that has the same, or almost the same, meaning as another word. An antonym has the opposite meaning. Write *S* if the word after each sentence is a synonym for the underlined word, or *A* if the word is an antonym of the underlined word. The first one is completed.

_____ 1. The woman's brave voice did not <u>quiver</u> when she gave the order.   shake

_____ 2. The <u>eldest</u> son was admired by his little brothers and sisters.   youngest

_____ 3. The <u>courier</u> carried important information to the general.   messenger

_____ 4. The women <u>devised</u> a successful plan to capture the information   forgot

_____ 5. The soldiers were <u>sullen</u> after they had been beaten   happy

_____ 6. "You lost the pouch?" Mrs. Martin said with <u>mock</u> surprise.   real

Story Facts and Ideas

Write at least one fact from the story to prove the following statements.

1. The Martin women were very brave.

2. The Loyalists hated the Martin family.

3. The British were winning the war in the South.

4. The Martin women were good actors.

5. The Martins were real American Patriots.

AMERICA'S WAR FOR INDEPENDENCE

Questions to Talk and Write About

1. Why was the Martin farm a dangerous place in which to live during the Revolutionary War?

2. Why did Grace and Rachel dress up like men when they met the British courier?

3. The Martin women cared for a wounded Continental soldier. They bravely captured important information from the British. How else might they have helped the American Patriots?

4. How do you think the Martins learned that the British courier would be coming? What might his messages have said?

5. This story is about the Martin women who helped fight the British. The story "A Time for Courage" tells how Abigail Adams helped as well. Compare the Martin women with Abigail Adams. In what different ways did they help win the Revolutionary War?

Things to Do

1. Select a scene from this story and write a script for a short play based on the scene. The scene may be about the Martin men leaving for war, the women making plans to fool the courier, the attack itself, or the scene at the house afterward.

2. Write a letter that Grace or Rachel might have written to her husband about her adventure.

3. Other women found ways to take part in the War for Independence. Make a list of how they helped. Ask your librarian to help you find other stories of women in the Revolution.

The World Turned Upside Down

Why did the British military band play a song called "The World Turned Upside Down" while the army surrendered?

Major Richard Collins of the British Army sat in his tent working. From the west came the constant thunder of cannons. The Major scarcely heard the sound. He was studying lists of supplies, and he did not like what he saw. The British were running low on ammunition. Their lines would not be able to hold out much longer. Unless the Royal Navy came to their rescue, the battle—and the war— would be over. This year of 1781 could bring the Americans their independence.

The Major stood up from his camp table and stepped outside. The Virginia air was pleasantly warm even though it was the middle of October. He gazed at the golden sunlight that filtered through the brilliant colors of the fall leaves. He wondered if the Virginia climate was always so mild.

This peaceful scene seemed a strange setting for what was happening. The British were trapped here on the end of a peninsula on the Virginia coast. In front of them, Washington's artillery pounded at their defenses day after day. With Washington's Continental Army were thousands of militia. In addition, the colonists were aided by the largest French army the Major had seen in America.

Collins turned and looked out on the Chesapeake Bay. The sea had always been Britain's ally in this war. British ships had always been there with their heavy cannons blasting the enemy. They brought supplies and fresh troops. But the ships he saw blocking the coast now were not British. They were French.

Major Collins still could not believe how quickly this had happened. A few weeks earlier,

---

"This has been a strange war from the start."

---

the British had seemed in control. They had marched into Virginia after a series of hard battles. They needed time to reorganize while they were waiting for the Royal Navy to arrive from New York. With fresh supplies and more troops, the British forces would move on.

Instead, they suddenly found themselves in this trap. Off the coast were thirty French warships, carrying three thousand marines. And at the same moment, Washington's Continentals and their French allies were moving in by land. The British were trapped by land and by sea. There was no way out.

The Major's closest friend, Captain James Rutledge, joined him. Rutledge was an artillery officer. He had just slept through a night and a day after nearly a week without sleep. His face still looked drawn and pale.

"How goes it, Colly?" he asked lightly. "Have the Americans and French started their retreat yet?"

"That's a poor joke, James," Collins said. "I think General Cornwallis will have to surrender."

Rutledge became serious. "Aye, we have little choice," he said. "Washington has been hammering at us for three weeks now. I think the General will surrender soon rather than see more lives lost."

This was the first time the two friends had talked of defeat. Collins felt better now that it was out in the open.

"This has been a strange war from the start," he said. "All day I have been wondering how I can explain it to my grandchildren when I am old. How did the most powerful nation in the world lose out to a band of ragged rebels?"

"Maybe I should not say this," Captain Rutledge replied slowly. "But in truth, Colly, I do not think we ever had a chance of winning."

The Major had sometimes had the same feeling. "But why, James?" he insisted. "We have always had them outnumbered. We controlled the seas. We have a well-trained army with the best equipment. Remember when we took the city of Charleston last year? We handed the Patriots the worst beating of the entire war. And yet here we are facing defeat. How do you explain that?"

They stopped talking as a column of Redcoats marched past. The weary men were on their way to the front lines. As the column moved on, Captain Rutledge explained his view of the war.

"Charleston is a perfect example of why we are losing," he said. "We did beat them badly. And we captured the only real city in the South. But then what happened? Patriots began appearing out of nowhere. They came from every farm and hamlet in the South."

"That's right," the Major said. "They did grow stronger after we took Charleston."

"Look at it this way, Colly," Rutledge continued. "At one time or another, we captured every city in America. We still have New York. Earlier we had Boston, then it was Philadelphia. Here in the

South, we took Savannah in Georgia and then Charleston. It never made any difference."

The Major had not thought of it that way before. He had been involved in taking every one of those cities, except Boston. It always seemed like an important step in defeating the Patriots. But Rutledge was right. Capturing those cities had not helped.

"I see what you mean," Collins said. "In Europe, when we captured another country's capital or its large cities, it meant victory. Remember how we thought Washington would surrender after we captured New York? We didn't realize that the Patriots' real strength was out in the farms and the villages."

"Exactly," Rutledge said. "And whenever we tried to move through the countryside, the Americans had the advantage. They could strike at us when and where we least expected it. Then they would simply melt away into the forests or the farmland. We weren't prepared for that kind of fighting."

They talked about how well those tactics had worked against them in the South. At first, the British forces had swept through Georgia and South Carolina. With help from powerful bands of Loyalists, victory seemed within their grasp.

But the Southern militia forces, with help from the Continental Army, had stopped them. For a year now, the British Army had steadily been weakened by small units of Patriot soldiers striking and then disappearing.

Captain Rutledge asked, "Who is that fellow who is so good at those hit-and-run tactics, the one they call 'The Swamp Fox?' Fighting him was like chasing a ghost."

Yorktown and the End of the War. Howard Pyle's 1881 view of the surrender of Yorktown.

"His name is Francis Marion," Collins said. "His secret was knowing his way through the swamps and the forests."

They fell silent when they saw a young lieutenant running toward them. He had orders for both of them to report to headquarters at once. They both knew something important was about to happen.

Headquarters for General Cornwallis were in a farmhouse outside the village of Yorktown. The lieutenant led them through two rooms crowded with clerks and officers into the General's office. They were surprised to see Cornwallis lying on a cot. He told them he was suffering from a fever.

"You two gentlemen have been on my staff for a long time," he said to them. "I am going to ask you to carry out the most difficult order I have ever given."

Collins knew at once what the order would be. He was certain Rutledge did, too. Both said they would obey any command he gave.

"I want you to ride out under a flag of truce," Cornwallis said. "Tell General Washington we are ready to surrender. We will turn over our weapons the morning after next. The Battle of Yorktown is over. And so, I suspect, is the war."

A few minutes later, with an escort of a dozen cavalry, the two friends rode out of camp. As they reached their own defenses, Captain Rutledge unfurled the white flag. The Redcoats nearest them stopped firing immediately. Then, like a ripple spreading out across a pool, the silence swept over the British lines. Moments later, the guns fell silent on the American side.

Rutledge and Collins were met by a group of Continentals in front of the American defenses. They delivered their message to a General Lincoln who received them politely and then rode back to camp.

The next day was spent in preparing weapons and packing equipment and clothing. The Major

found that he did not feel like talking to anyone, not even Rutledge. It was many years since Great Britain had lost a war, and he found that defeat had a bitter taste.

On the morning of October 19, 1781, Collins and Rutledge led the first two columns of British Redcoats onto the battlefield to surrender. The British soldiers passed between two lines a half a mile long. One line was made up of the Americans in their worn, tattered uniforms. The other line was the French army sent to help the Americans. The French soldiers were wearing splendid green uniforms. One by one, the British then stacked their weapons in an open field.

Behind them, Collins heard the Continental band start playing "Yankee Doodle." From their own camp came the sounds of the British band playing a popular English song. Collins and Rutledge could not help grinning when they heard it. "Listen, James," the Major said. "Recognize that song?"

Rutledge laughed. "Everyone knows it. And what could be a better song to play at a time like this?"

The tune the British band was playing was "The World Turned Upside Down."

STORY NOTES

The conversation between Collins and Rutledge was made up to tell about the British surrender at Yorktown. All the other events are real. After Cornwallis's surrender the bands did play "Yankee Doodle" and "The World Turned Upside Down."

The British continued to fight elsewhere but realized that they had lost the war. They had underestimated the strength of the colonists and the difficulty of fighting so far from home. The treaty signed in 1783 gave the Americans all the land from the east coast to the Mississippi River.

AMERICA'S WAR FOR INDEPENDENCE

Word Study

Fill in the blank in each of the following sentences with the correct word from the list. Then use the numbers to find the hidden message.

artillery	scarcely	tactics
hamlet	grasp	truce
peninsula	Swamp Fox	unfurled

1. The soldier was so tired that he could __ __ __ __ __ __ __ __ stand up.
  1 2 3 4 2 5 6 7

2. Another name for a small town is a __ __ __ __ __ __ .
  8 3 9 6 5 10

3. Washington's __ __ __ __ __ __ __ __ __ wore down the British defenses.
  3 4 10 15 6 6 5 4 7

4. The Americans trapped the British at the end of a __ __ __ __ __ __ __ __ __ .
  19 5 12 15 12 1 11 6 3

5. The Captain __ __ __ __ __ __ __ __ a white flag.
  11 12 16 11 4 6 5 13

6. The British __ __ __ __ __ __ __ did not work.
  10 3 2 10 15 2 1

7. Victory seemed within their __ __ __ __ __ .
  17 4 3 1 19

8. The British officer had a flag of __ __ __ __ __ when he surrendered.
  10 4 11 2 5

9. The British called Francis Marion "The __ __ __ __ __   __ __ __ ."
  1 18 3 9 19   16 22 20

The hidden message:

__ __ __   __ __ __ __ __   __ __ __ __ __ __
10 8 5   18 22 4 6 13   10 11 4 12 5 13

__ __ __ __ __ __   __ __ __ __
11 19 1 15 13 5   13 22 18 12

AMERICA'S WAR FOR INDEPENDENCE

Story Facts and Ideas

Explain the meaning of the following quotations from the story.

1. Collins: "How did the most powerful nation in the world lose out to a band of ragged rebels?"

2. Rutledge: "At one time or another, we captured every city in America. . . . It never made any difference."

3. Cornwallis: "I am going to ask you to carry out the most difficult order I have ever given."

4. Rutledge: "And what could be a better song to play at a time like this?"

Questions to Talk and Write About

1. What type of man was Major Collins? List and describe his qualities. Give examples of his actions that show these qualities.

2. What made the British so certain they would win the war?

3. The British thought that capturing American cities would make the Patriots surrender. What went wrong with their plan?

4. Explain General Washington's plan at the battle of Yorktown. Why was the strategy so successful? Describe the part that the French played.

5. Why did the British officers smile when they heard their band playing "The World Turned Upside Down"? Why do you think the author chose that title for this story?

Things to Do

1. Imagine that Major Collins kept a journal. Write two or three paragraphs that he might have written when he returned to his tent after the surrender.

2. The American band played "Yankee Doodle." The British band played "The World Turned Upside Down." Use the library to find out more about songs that were played and sung during the Revolution. Find the words to some of these songs.

3. Write a newspaper article that might have appeared in an American newspaper in 1781. Tell what happened at Yorktown and what it meant for America.

Toward a More Perfect Union

Why did the farmers of Massachusetts rebel in 1786?

Background

The years following the American Revolution were not easy ones. The new national government was weak, and the states were like thirteen little countries, constantly bickering with one another. Every state made its own money, confusing people until the money was considered worthless. Many people lost their farms, businesses, and jobs.

Our story begins three years after the peace treaty with Britain was signed.

Part 1.
Troubled Times, Winter 1786–1787

Daniel Shays wanted only to be left alone to farm his land. But on this blustery day in December, 1786, he saw that he could not stay out of the trouble that was brewing.

The four men seated around his kitchen table were his friends and his neighbors. Like many farmers all over New England, they were in

trouble. They had come to him for help. They were losing their farms because they could not pay their debts. He could see in their eyes the look of men who were beaten and desperate. How could he turn them away?

"All right," Shays said. "I will help. What is it you want of me?" Around the table smiles appeared on the pale, unshaven faces. He knew why they had come to him. He had been a captain in the Continental Army during the War for Independence. Many farmers had served under him, and they still called him Captain Shays.

"We just want you to lead us, Cap'n," Jed Waters said. "Every time a Massachusetts court meets, another family loses their farm for unpaid taxes. How can we stop this?"

Bands of farmers had already armed themselves and surrounded a few courthouses. The judges could not get through to try cases. But now the governor had called out the state militia. The farmers did not know what to do. They hoped Shays would have a solution.

"I believe we have been pushed into this," Shays said. "But I want you to understand one thing. We cannot win. When we take up arms, we will be outlaws, not Patriots. The Massachusetts militia will use cannons to blast us right out of the state."

"That's what they said when we took on the Redcoats twelve years ago," Luke Appleton said. "And we're kind of hoping the militia boys won't favor shooting their neighbors."

Shays knew it was useless to argue. They would fight whether he led them or not. He told them he needed time to think. He pulled on his coat and stepped outside. He tried to think of some way to avoid a massacre. Instead, he found himself thinking of how hard these years were on all of them.

Like the others, Shays had trudged home from the war without a penny. In his pocket, he carried a paper from the Congress promising to pay him

for his Army time. But the paper turned out to be worthless. Congress had no money. The states had refused to grant the national government the power to raise money through taxes.

Shays had figured he would forget about the pay. As long as he could farm, he thought, he could feed his family.

The refusal of the states to give Congress real power caused even worse problems. Farmers found they could no longer sell their products in England or the West Indies. Those had been their largest markets. But Congress did not have the power to make new trade agreements. Instead, farm prices fell lower and lower. It hardly paid a family to bring in the harvest.

Worst of all the problems were the state taxes. Massachusetts taxes had gone sky-high, but the farmers had no money to pay them. They began borrowing just to pay their tax bills. Then they could not repay the loans. Shays himself had almost been sent to prison because he could not pay a merchant twelve dollars. He would never forget the shame of standing in that courtroom.

Others had put up their crops or farm animals to guarantee a loan. Many took a mortgage on their farms. When they could not pay their debts, the judges ordered the property seized. Many times Shays had seen the sheriff's men leading away a farmer's dairy herd. By this winter of 1786, hundreds had lost their farms.

Daniel Shays made up his mind. He went back into the kitchen and told them his plan.

"Round up as many men as you can," he said. "We will march on the arsenal at Springfield. If we can seize guns, ammunition, and cannons, we will have a slim chance to win our demands. A thousand well-armed farmers may persuade the governor to yield. We will make only two demands of the governor. One is to have more time to pay our debts. The other is to be allowed to use crops to pay our taxes."

A NEW BEGINNING

Detail of engraving of Shays' Rebellion. The Bettmann Archive

Luke pounded his fist on the table. "That's just what we need, Captain. We can show the people of this state that we have rights that cannot be ignored."

Three weeks later, in January 1787, they were ready. With eleven hundred farmers behind him, Shays led the march on Springfield.

The Massachusetts militia were ready for them. Shays felt sick when he saw the cannons aimed at the farmers. A moment later, the cannons fired into the farmers' lines. Shays never had a chance to give an order. The men turned and fled in all directions. Four of the farmers lay dead in the snow.

The militia rounded up some of the men. Shays and a few others escaped to Vermont. Most returned quietly to their homes. Shays' Rebellion was over, but it had shocked the new nation into action. If something wasn't done soon, they might have another revolution on their hands. It was

time to write a new constitution that gave the national government the power to do what was needed.

Story Facts and Ideas I

Write short answers to these questions.

1. WHO took part in the Rebellion?

2. WHEN did the story take place?

3. WHERE did the action happen?

4. WHAT did Shays and the others do?

5. WHY did the farmers believe they had to resort to violence?

A NEW BEGINNING

Part 2.
"We the People," Spring 1788

Dancer, Jonathan's speedy Morgan mare, was saddled and ready to go. The horse stamped one hoof impatiently. Rebecca had tied Jonathan's pack behind the saddle.

The horse was ready, but Jonathan did not feel so eager. A month earlier, it had been easy to announce boldly, "I am going to go to Boston to speak to the Massachusetts Convention. The United States must have a new government, or we will have more and more rebellions like Shays'. We farmers must show that we favor the constitution, or Massachusetts may vote against it."

But now the thought of speaking to three hundred and fifty state delegates filled him with fear. He had spoken often in Town Meeting. But that was with friends and neighbors. The idea of speaking before the State Convention made his legs feel wobbly.

Rebecca sensed his uneasiness. "Jonathan Smith," she said, "all you have to do is put your foot in the stirrup and swing yourself up. Once you are on your way, you will feel your confidence grow."

He knew that she was right. He swung himself into the saddle and bolted out of the farmyard. With luck, he could be in Boston in three days.

The constitution had been written a year earlier at a convention in Philadelphia. Some of the great leaders of the Revolution had helped to write it. General Washington had been president of the Convention. Dr. Benjamin Franklin at the age of eighty-one had added important ideas. Now it was up to the people of each state to accept, or ratify, the new constitution.

Every town in Massachusetts had copies of the document. Jonathan had brought one home and studied it with Rebecca. It seemed to correct all the weaknesses of the old Congress.

"I like the way the government is divided into three branches," Rebecca had said. "Congress makes laws for the nation; a president sees that the laws are carried out; and courts handle disputes. No single branch can become too powerful."

As Jonathan rode, he thought about how much he and Rebecca liked the proposed new government. He recalled, too, how shocked they had been to learn that most of their neighbors were

"... I have known the worth of good government by the want of it."

opposed to the constitution. Mr. Chase, the owner of the trading post, had said, "We fought a war for independence to get rid of a tyrant. This constitution would simply turn the national government into a new tyrant."

"Aye, that is true," Lucas Waring, a farmer, said. "They say George Washington will be the first president. We may as well call him King George— as much a tyrant as England's King George was."

Jonathan and others had argued for the constitution. Nancy Pelham had declared, "The government we have now is simply not a government. Each state goes its own way. Each state even prints its own money. My uncle has some Delaware money for twenty kegs of molasses he sold. And what good is it? No merchant in Massachusetts will accept that Delaware paper."

No one seemed to change anyone's mind. Even after Jonathan left for Boston, men and women were arguing about the constitution in every town he passed through.

Jonathan made his way through the streets of Boston and took a room at an inn. The next day he found himself in the Meeting Hall facing a crowd of over three hundred delegates. When his name was called, Jonathan stood up and faced the great crowd.

"Mr. President, I am a plain man," he began. He was pleased that his voice sounded clear and strong. "I get my living by the plow. I am not used to speaking in public, but I beg your leave to say a few words."

Jonathan was surprised to see that the delegates were listening carefully.

"I live in a part of the country where I have known the worth of good government by the want of it. Shays' Rebellion took place near our home. Had there been a strong national government, those men would not have been driven to rebellion.

"When I saw this constitution, I found that it was a cure for the old disorders. I got a copy of it. My wife and I read it over and over. We thought well of the balance among three branches of the government. We did not go to any lawyer to ask an opinion. We have no lawyer in our town, and we do well enough without one. My wife and I formed our own opinion, and we are pleased with this constitution. If we are ever to be a united country, we should favor this new government."

Jonathan stopped and sat down. He felt as if he had been talking for hours. There was a moment of silence. Then, suddenly, about half the delegates stood and applauded.

Jonathan stayed in Boston for two more days until the vote was taken—187 delegates voted in favor; 168 were opposed. A few hours later,

Jonathan was heading back to western Massachusetts. The vote had been very close. Jonathan could not help but wonder if he had helped to change anyone's vote.

Story Facts and Ideas II

Write short answers to these questions.

1. WHO was the main character in this story?

2. WHEN did the story take place?

3. WHERE was the Massachusetts Convention held?

4. WHAT did Jonathan do?

5. WHY did he do this?

STORY NOTES

Daniel Shays and Jonathan Smith were real people. We can only guess about things they said. But Jonathan's speech was written down, and you have read it almost exactly as he gave it. For some time following the rebellion, Daniel Shays would be considered an outlaw. Then he was pardoned and in his old age received a federal pension.

A NEW BEGINNING

Word Study

Use the clues to complete the following crossword puzzle. (puzzle words: arsenal, blustery, Boston, constitution, convention, Daniel, debts, delegate, farmers, tyrant, herd, mortgage, plow, rebellion, stirrup, yield)

ACROSS

2. fight against a government or ruler
5. a set of rules of government
6. one who rules with absolute power
8. to give in or surrender
10. Many farmers had to _____ their crops back into the ground.
11. people who asked Shays to help them
12. windy and chilly
14. a loan for a house or farm
15. Shays' first name

DOWN

1. a person who represents others
3. where the Massachusetts Convention was held
4. part of a saddle that supports the feet
5. a meeting where people discuss common problems
7. money that people owe
9. a place where military equipment is kept
13. many animals together

Questions to Talk and Write About

1. "When we take up arms," Daniel Shays said, "we will be outlaws, not Patriots." "That's what they said when we took on the Redcoats," Luke replied. What did Daniel and Luke mean? Compare Shays' Rebellion with the War for Independence.

2. Why did the United States need a new constitution in 1788, only seven years after the country had won its independence?

3. What was the main idea of the new constitution? Why did some people like this? Why were other people afraid?

4. Compare Daniel Shays and Jonathan Smith. In what ways were they alike? How were they different?

5. Why did the author name this story "Toward a More Perfect Union"?

Things to Do

1. Write a brief newspaper story about each event—Shays' Rebellion and Jonathan Smith's speech to the Massachusetts Legislature.

2. Imagine this scene: Daniel Shays dines at the home of Jonathan and Rebecca Smith. Jonathan has just returned home from the Massachusetts convention. What do you think Daniel, Rebecca, and Jonathan would say to one another? Plan to act out the scene.

3. The 1787 Constitution is the one we live with today. Write a brief report about the Constitutional Convention of 1787 in Philadelphia.

A NEW BEGINNING

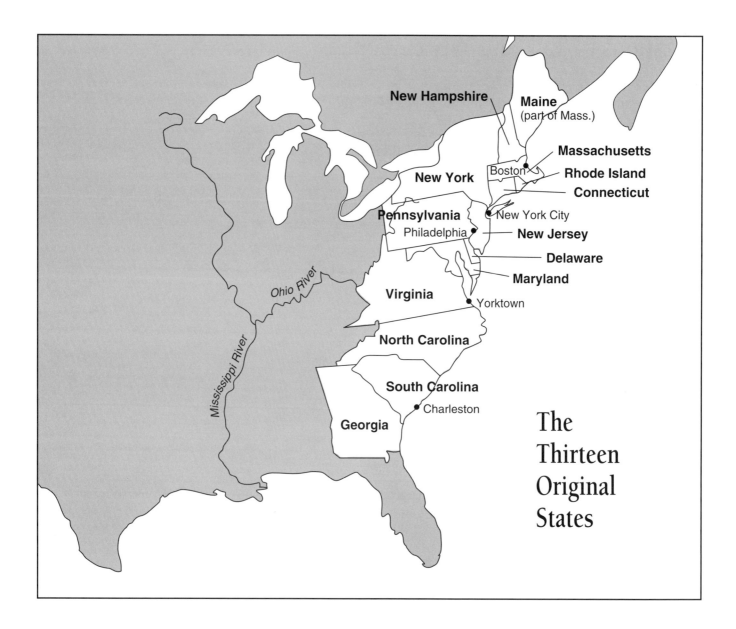

The
Thirteen
Original
States

A NEW BEGINNING

Over the Next Hill

Why was harvest day so important to Elizabeth and Jeremy?

It was harvest time in the year 1790. The first harvest on our own farm!

Jeremy and I had just finished storing baskets of apples in the root cellar. We paused to survey the fields while the children ran to feed some apple parings and other scraps of food to the pigs. The fields of wheat, oats, barley, and corn were bathed in the orange glow of the setting sun. The crops looked rich and full. We felt proud of all we had coaxed from the rocky Vermont soil.

Our neighbors would be coming the next day to help with the harvest. We had invited everyone in the area of our village. That was the tradition we had grown up with in Connecticut. If Vermonters followed the same tradition, many would come. In return, we would provide them with the finest feast we could manage.

"It would be easier to plan if I knew how many were coming," Jeremy said.

Just then we heard the sound of horses approaching. We turned to look down the dirt lane that led to the village. A moment later two riders appeared over the crest of the hill.

A NEW BEGINNING

"However many are coming," I said, giving Jeremy a joyful hug, "plan on two more. Here come Ben and Lynda, right on time."

Ben and Lynda Collier were my two closest friends. We had received a brief letter from Lynda a week earlier. She had said they were coming up from Connecticut to help with our first harvest. We had not seen either of them for two years.

Ben and Lynda galloped into the yard and leaped off their horses. Chickens, ducks, and geese scattered noisily in all directions. We had a grand reunion on the spot, with hugs, kisses, handshakes, and moist eyes.

The children came forward and offered shy greetings to "Uncle Ben" and "Aunt Lynda."

That evening we stuffed ourselves with venison stew, fresh brown bread, and apple cider. Dessert was an apple cobbler topped with thick cream. Everything we ate that night came from our land. That is one of the great rewards of farming. With this harvest, we hoped the farm would now supply nearly all our needs.

Over supper, we caught up on each other's news. We had seen little of our friends in recent years, and there was much to talk about. I had grown up with Ben and Lynda. When the War for Independence started, Lynda and I had joined the Daughters of Liberty, and Ben and Jeremy had joined the Connecticut militia together. We were seventeen at the time. After the war, Lynda and Ben were married. Jeremy and I were wed a little more than a year later.

All four of us had planned to own our own farms. But the years after the war had been hard ones, especially for farmers. Ben had been working on his father's farm and trying to save money. Lynda worked at a printer's shop. Now Jeremy and I had become the first to achieve the dream of buying a farm.

Our friends had only a quick look at the farm in the fading light. I asked them how they liked it.

Just like old times, they answered the question by teasing.

"Well, Elizabeth," Ben began, pretending to be very serious. "We were wondering how you and Jeremy had chosen Vermont. I heard that there was only one acre of topsoil for the whole state."

Lynda kept the same mock serious tone. "And don't they say that a grasshopper crossing a Vermont field carries his own dinner?"

We could not help but laugh, and the children quickly joined in.

"Is it true," Ben wanted to know, "that the pigs are so thin it takes two to cast one shadow?"

They had saved up a dozen more of these comments. Each one set off new bursts of laughter until tears rolled down our cheeks. I had my hands full quieting the children when it was time for bed. Once they were tucked in for the night, we took Ben and Lynda into the parlor. With cups of tea and a crackling fire, we settled down to talk.

We talked a little about how much better conditions were under the new constitution. The national government was strong enough to straighten out the problems that followed the war. Farming and trade were thriving again. And, with George Washington as our first president, everyone felt a new sense of confidence.

All this time, Jeremy and I had been wondering what Ben and Lynda were up to. It did not seem likely they would make this long journey only to help with our harvest.

"Ben," Jeremy said suddenly, "if this is harvest time, why are you not working your father's fields?"

They both seemed caught off guard. Ben laughed and said, "Elizabeth Cooper, your husband is a clever man. I do believe Jeremy is on to us."

"The fact is," Lynda confessed, "we have both spent the past six months planning an expedition. We are heading west—to Ohio. We will be leaving in early spring."

A NEW BEGINNING

"We want you two and your little ones to join us," Ben said.

Now it was our turn to be surprised. Jeremy and I stared at each other, trying to get used to this bold proposal.

Ben and Lynda kept right on talking with growing excitement. Nearly fifty families had signed up, they told us. Arrangements had already been made with a land company for a large tract. The land was on both sides of a small river that flowed into the Ohio. The price was so low that some families planned to start with 200-acre farms.

"This will not be like blazing trails in the wilderness," Lynda said. "Thousands have removed to Ohio already."

"Like Jeremy and me," Ben added, "most of the men are veteran Continentals. We will have a skilled militia if there is any trouble."

We talked about the plan far into the night. Jeremy and I had often talked about heading west. We knew the river valleys of Ohio were as rich as any farmland in America. A family could manage a much larger farm there and even hire two or three men to help with the work. It would be far different from farming the stubborn, thin soil of New England. And when our two children grew up, there would be plenty of land to share with them.

On our own, we had not been willing to take the risk. We did not want to become pioneers while our children were so young. But this expedition made it seem far safer. It was a far grander dream than our small Vermont farm. All night the same question made sleep difficult for both of us. Should we leave everything and join this Ohio expedition?

Harvest day answered our question.

With the first streaks of morning light, our neighbors began to arrive. They came over the hills from every direction. A few were on horseback. Some walked, carrying sickles, threshers, flails, and other tools on their shoulders. But most came on the back of farm wagons pulled by horses or oxen.

With help from Lynda and our six-year-old daughter, I had tea ready for any who wanted it. There were also warm doughnuts or biscuits with honey. Almost everyone passed through the kitchen. They introduced themselves and enjoyed the early breakfast. A few of the women stayed

Farming and trade were thriving again.

there to help with the cooking. The rest joined the men and the children heading for the fields.

We had a grand harvest day. For much of the year, farm life demands long hours of hard toil. From the spring thaw until autumn, every moment of daylight must be used wisely. Harvest time is different. True, there is work to be done. But the labor of many hands can complete a harvest in a few hours. Mixed with the work is a sense of fun and celebration.

By the time the sun had risen above the eastern hills, the harvest was well underway. I counted forty men and women before I lost track. There were also scores of children of all ages, a few working, most playing. Within an hour of the time we started, the first loaded wagon pulled up at the root cellar. It was piled high with pumpkins and squashes.

Clusters of people were at work in every field. The sound of laughter and of songs rang through the hills. A group of about twenty teenage boys and girls took over the corn harvest. They sat facing each other in two rows, husking the corn and filling basket after basket. They sang and joked

A NEW BEGINNING

constantly. I noticed, too, that they played a game I remembered well. The boy who husks a red ear is allowed to kiss the girl next to him.

By afternoon, the root cellar and the barn were packed with our crops. We would be able to sell or trade even more than I had counted on. There was even plenty for a special birthday present I wanted for Jeremy. I would trade with the livery man to buy a new saddle for him to use.

Lynda and Ben had used some planking stored in the barn to make a long harvest table. They set it up in the yard near the kitchen door, and I set out the meal with the help of the other women. Chicken and wild turkey, roasted or boiled, a smoked ham, roast pork, meat pie and fruit pies, puddings, and fruit. There were also jugs of cider and smaller jugs of rum to mix with water.

People talked quietly and enjoyed the meal. Other dishes would be set out later. Then the first

two fiddlers tuned up and started playing. The young people, with their endless energy, immediately formed lines for dancing. The party was just beginning. After sundown, we would go indoors for more refreshments, songs, and dancing.

Jeremy and I moved away from the others to go look at our harvest. His face seemed to glow with the pleasure of the day. "This is what we always dreamed of, Elizabeth," he said, smiling. "The day seems even more perfect because it is our farm and our harvest."

"And our neighbors," I added. "I feel like we are already part of the community."

Jeremy nodded and put his arm in mine. "Do you think Ohio could be more beautiful or offer greater joys?"

Several times during the day I had asked myself that same question. By now, we had both reached the same answer. "I don't think Ohio

America's Story

A NEW BEGINNING

could ever be better than this," I said. "There is always the idea that just over the next hill there might be a bigger farm, a better farm. But we have what we were looking for. I think that's enough for now."

The great harvest moon was shining in the sky. We turned and walked back toward the others.

STORY NOTES

Elizabeth and Jeremy are not real people. But there were many people like them who had to decide whether or not to move farther west for the promise of more land. Leaving home was a difficult decision that often meant leaving one's family and friends behind—perhaps never to see them again—for a rugged life in the wilderness. Nevertheless, many saw the move west as a great opportunity and an exciting adventure. This led to the settlement of states such as Tennessee, Kentucky, Ohio, Illinois, Indiana, and Michigan—and new problems with Native Americans.

In 1790, most people lived on farms as Elizabeth and Jeremy did. Philadelphia was the nation's largest city with 42,000 people. It had only just started to lay sidewalks, and many of its streets were still made of cobblestones or dirt. Having one's own farm was still the dream of most Americans.

Word Study

Here is a list of words from this story, along with a list of definitions. Read each definition. Write the word before the correct definition. Then write your own sentence using the word. (Two of the words have no definitions listed.)

| cobbler | flail | propose | toil | tract | thriving |
| planking | husking | sickle | thresher | tradition | venison |

1. _____ to suggest an idea

2. _____ several thick boards

3. _____ meat from a deer; used for food

4. _____ hard work; labor

5. _____ a deep-dish pie; also, a person who fixes shoes

6. _____ a sharp tool used for cutting wheat

7. _____ old custom handed down from parents to children

8. _____ very successful; growing and increasing

9. _____ a large area of land

10. _____ removing the covering from ears of corn

A NEW BEGINNING

Story Facts and Ideas

Complete the following sentences.

1. Lynda and Ben visited their friends in Vermont because

2. Elizabeth and Jeremy liked farming because

3. Neighbors were important at harvest time because

4. Elizabeth and Jeremy had a successful harvest because their farm and root cellar were filled with

5. The Coopers decided not to go west because

Questions to Talk and Write About

1. What changes had taken place in the lives of Elizabeth, Jeremy, Ben, and Lynda since the War for Independence? What changes had taken place in the American government?

2. Why was the harvest an especially happy time for the early American farmers?

3. What reasons did Ben and Lynda have for wanting to move to Ohio? How would farming there be different? In what ways would it be the same as in Vermont?

4. List the qualities that an early American farmer needed. In what ways did Elizabeth and Jeremy show these qualities?

5. Explain Jeremy and Elizabeth's reasons for staying in Vermont.

Things to Do

1. Add a new ending. This story ends with Jeremy and Elizabeth walking back to the harvest celebration. Have them tell Ben and Lynda about their decision. Include what their two friends might say. Have them announce their decision to their neighbors.

2. Do some research on early American farming. See if you can find drawings of early farming tools such as the flail, the thresher, and the sickle. Prepare a brief report to share with the class.

3. Imagine that you are one of the Cooper children. What would you say to convince your parents to stay in Vermont or to go to Ohio?

4. Write a letter that Ben or Lynda might have written from Ohio to Jeremy and Elizabeth ten years later.